THE BIG MAN
THE JOHN WAYNE STORY

THE BIG MAN

THE JOHN WAYNE STORY

Mike Tomkies

Arthur Barker Limited
5 Winsley Street London W1

792·091
WHYNE

SBN 2 13 00342 2/7203

Printed in Great Britain by
Willmer Brothers Limited, Birkenhead

CONTENTS

FOREWORD

Shortly before Duke Wayne won the Oscar for *True Grit* I was invited for lunch at his sea front home in Newport Beach, California, and we were whiling away an hour by walking through his personal picture gallery. They told their own story, those pictures. Yellowing shots of a slim and rangy young Duke from the last days of the silent movies with semi-forgotten cowboy stars like Harry Carey and Smith Bellew. 'Yeah, I was a real skinny guy then,' he laughs in that voice of his that seems to boom up from some deep cellar. 'For years I rode or staggered over most of the mountains west of Denver, doing my own stunts for eatin' money.' Shots of Wayne with stars like Victor McLaglen, Clark Gable, Gary Cooper, Tracy and other great stars of the past, all dead and gone now. And with others who were going to be great stars fifteen years ago but never quite made it.

Yet here was Duke, the last of the super-stars, who in a forty-years' career has been voted the world's most popular actor more times than any star living or dead, jabbing away with a huge finger and telling outrageously true anecdotes as each picture prompted something in his memory. It seemed to me the whole of motion picture history was with us in that hall. The images of an extraordinary man's life.

Suddenly Duke paused before a picture of his two strapping sons Michael and Patrick striding along where he, taller than either of them at six feet four, was walking in front with that familiar cutting-in action of his right arm. He looked good in the picture, a big proud and cocky grin on his face.

'Gee, that was ten years ago. I wish to God I looked like that now,' he said. 'Not for myself but because of my work. The kind of parts I can play. I'd still like to play romantic leads y'know but hell, how can I at my age? I long ago gave up roles where I win beautiful women. A man has to know when to stop.'

He patted the slight paunch that protruded from the massive 244-lb Wayne physique. The granitic face saddened. 'Godammit, I hate getting old. You just can't do what you used to any more. I hurt this damn shoulder when I fell from that horse out in Louisiana. In the old days it would have taken ten days or two weeks to heal up but it's now more than a month and it's still giving me hell.'

He pounded a fist into his palm and for a brief instant I saw his hands as if stilled in a movie shot. Huge hands, gnarled like the burls on a snag-born fir. They have a life of their own, those hands.

It was a moment where the legend seemed to separate from reality, when Wayne's dualism came suddenly into focus. For that instant John Wayne, who it seems has been for ever linked in our minds with bloody wars, floods, fires, doomed boats and planes and gun and fist fights, a man who licked cancer in real life, was beneath it all strangely vulnerable. Like all men whose lives have been filled with action he wanted, if only for that moment, to have his youth back. But he was out of the mood immediately and regaling me with more of the stories behind the photographs.

When his beautiful Peruvian wife Pilar called him away to take a phone call, I went out and sat on his sun-filled patio, looking out over the cerulean sea which fills the Waynes' view of the whole of Newport harbour. I'd no intention then of writing a book about him, just a magazine series, but both Duke and Pilar had given me freely of their time and I'd spent many hours with them.

As I sat there in the sun after my long drive from Canada where I was then living, I became lost in reverie, thinking of the John Wayne who rode through the dreams of my childhood, as he may have done through yours. The Homeric mythical, superman hero who becomes real in the memory. In the whitecaps out there I saw him again, red-scarved and bawling orders from the deck in *Wake Of The Red Witch*, the homesick young sailor in *The Long Voyage Home*, skippering the little torpedo boats in *They Were Expendable* with the Jap shells falling dangerously close. On the sand by his jetty where he now busied his off-screen moments teaching his little four-year-old daughter Marisa to swim, I saw him again but now on the *Sands of Iwo Jima* when he was the big tough sergeant bullying his rookie Marines to manhood. His green sprinkled lawns became now the ould sod of Ireland where in *The Quiet Man* he'd gone seeking peace from pugilistic memories, only to find himself romancing colleen Maureen O'Hara and fighting what is probably the screen's greatest ever fist fight with his real life pal, the late lovable Victor McLaglen. 'Oh, tis the Marquis o' Queensberry rules is it!' roars McLaglen, belting Wayne before he's back on his feet, and off they go again, battling through bars and down the mountain side till that final lusty victory when all are pals and Wayne gets his girl.

An impossible figure really, perhaps, but Wayne has always consciously controlled his screen persona. 'I stay away from nuances and from psychoanalysts' couches,' he said once. 'Couches are good for one thing only and conflict is made to be won, not gone under to.' Before Wayne's hero there is no disillusioned 'anti'.

For me it's something more than memories too, for Wayne *is* a part of my youth, his films almost part of real experience. The tough, laconic decent-at-heart Ringo Kid in *Stagecoach* seeking to revenge his father's murder, the outspoken rebellious western sons of the early forties who'd grow up straight, provided they didn't get shot first. By the late forties he was already the father figure, the head scout or trail boss to a bunch of wild saddle tramps, or the lone man on a horse, my favourite image of all, hard and merciless with men who stepped out of line but shy with women, treating them all with rough backwoods courtesy.

'Hello there' was all he said to the girl as he rode down the mountains and up through the long grass. It was all he need say to that girl, the girl standing on the cabin porch, alighting from a train or in the canteen of a construction camp, for she was instantly drawn to that powerful sexual authority of which he never took advantage. Where had he come from, before the mountains and the long grass? We all wanted to know.

Wayne became part of our youthful dreams because, bewildered by life's early paradoxes and the decisions we had constantly to make between good and evil in our young lives, he suggested another world. A world of just and simple virtues where if a man had the courage to do what he had to do, he could live by his own code and one day ride away free with his girl to that bend in the bright flowing river where the tall pines combed the morning wind. Maybe that world never existed but we believe in it with all our hearts.

Today Wayne's acting has tremendous authority. He has become the personification of the West, its last generic star. He's as fit as any man could be at his age. One must remember that while he's a wealthy tycoon with many business interests apart from his acting, he spends as much time working out of doors as the average cowboy ever did.

The stories and apocrypha surrounding Wayne are legion. For years he was known as a man who could outdrink and out-talk any man in Hollywood. I can believe it. And in the past he *has* clipped a man or two down to size in real life. He once busted a man's jaw who pushed him too far. But today, after the loss of one lung to cancer, fathering and rearing seven children (he has no fewer than sixteen grandchildren), that elusive Oscar at last under his belt, plus the toll of advancing years – these have taken much of any earlier violence out of him. It is hard to find aggression in the mature and today Duke is a gentle man.

I had a glimpse of what Duke is like as a father when he and Pilar called me in to lunch. As we sat down to an enormous tuna salad, little Marisa started crying in the background. Her elder brother Ethan had taken her little brown book away from her, she said. Pilar told her it would be all right and they'd sort it out later but right now they were having lunch.

Marisa kept whimpering so Duke dropped his bread on the salad and got up to put things right. He established in fact that it *was* Ethan's notebook – he'd given it to him a few weeks earlier himself and it had Ethan's name on it. So Duke quietly told Marisa it was Ethan's and therefore she must be mistaken. He went into his study and got her another notebook with *her* name on it. Then he came back to his lunch. I don't think many fathers would have reacted like that.

Shortly afterwards Duke and Pilar's eldest daughter Aissa came in and said she wanted a haircut and set that afternoon. Duke asked 'Why?'

'Oh, it's awful – look!' said Aissa and she showed her father some little frayed ends of hair.

'Aissa, you *couldn't* look more beautiful than you do right now,' Duke said. But she got her money. And the delighted look on her face! At thirteen her appearance was very important.

As he polished off the last of his tuna, Duke's eyes twinkled. 'I think they thought my plate was Marisa's,' he said in a theatrical voice. The maid smiled but quickly emptied another tin on to Duke's plate and he soon put that away too. Afterwards we all drank Sanka, decaffeined coffee, and watched as Marisa ventured out into the garden. Pilar kept a watchful eye on her. 'That's the only trouble with living so near the water,' she said. 'You daren't let them out of your sight.'

I asked Duke if he'd mind posing for some pictures with Marisa and her little tricycle. Before he came out he put on a yachting cap to cover up his bald spot with a rueful grin. 'I don't care about it myself,' he said. 'Hell, it happens to a lot of men. But I don't see why I should inflict it upon other people!' It wasn't vanity because although he wears a small hairpiece for his films and public appearances, in his normal life he never bothers. He is able to regard the John Wayne persona with considerable detachment.

I've watched Duke at work on several films but I've never yet seen him get rattled or throw a fit of temperament as many top stars do if they think the occasion demands it. While he was making *The Undefeated* in the scorching heat at Baton Rouge, Louisiana, scores of rubber neckers and fans gate-crashed the location, all eager to talk to him and shake his hand. It's strange how a big star personality like Wayne's seems to bring out both the worst and best in people. Often he had to put up with the sort of tactless remark bordering on insult which a lesser man could not have borne without showing irritation. Some women actually told him how lousy he'd been in this and that picture. But no matter what they said Duke smiled and had a deft turn of phrase which kept the good humour.

If someone oversteps the mark too far, Wayne usually says nothing. Rude or kind, the fans are all part of the business he loves and have their definite place in the scheme of things. I heard one local farmer host refer to a cocktail party his daughter had organized at their home and Wayne politely agreed he'd enjoyed the do and made a compliment about the girl. The farmer accepted the compliment but then added some totally asinine crack to the effect that Wayne needn't get ideas about his daughter. Duke, who barely remembered the girl and had merely been trying to be polite, tightened his lips but said nothing. He knew that the man, in a misplaced attempt at familiarity, had lapsed into vulgarity and was immediately embarrassed about it, and he didn't want or need to add to the man's discomfiture.

Once a man shouted out from the crowd, asking if Wayne spoke Spanish.

'Not too well,' admitted Duke.

'What!' replied the man, anxious to show off his knowledge about Wayne, 'you've had three Spanish wives and you can't speak Spanish?'

'Waal,' drawled Duke, 'I guess I just never listened to 'em'. Loud laughter and collapse of bumptious party.

I really like Duke Wayne. That's why I wrote this book. It isn't meant to be a definitive biography – only Duke himself can write that and I hope he does. This is merely a portrait, an inadequate tribute perhaps, to a man I came to admire and respect.

1

THE PIONEER

To look at Duke Wayne in these later years you could be forgiven for imagining maybe the man had been hacked whole from the non-corrosive rock of the harsh Mojave desert where he spent much of his youth. Even his history is right for the legend. His background is as truly pioneer as any shown in his films.

Marion Michael Morrison – Duke's real name – was born on 26 May 1907 in the small town of Winterset, Iowa, where his father Clyde Morrison ran his own apothecary, the kind of chemist's shop long gone from the American country scene. 'Doc' Morrison, as he was fondly known, was of Scots-Irish descent and he handled minor first-aid cases himself, dispensed prescriptions and handed them out along with his own brand of homespun philosophy.

Duke's mother, Mary Margaret Brown, called Molly by her friends, was an attractive woman of pure Irish-blooded pioneer stock whose own mother had been born in Cork. She was a tiny woman, red-haired and vivacious, and Doc himself was not a giant. He was 5ft 11 ins tall but extremely well built, weighing some two hundred and ten pounds, and was darkly handsome. Apparently Duke inherits his huge physique from his mother's father who was 6 ft 3 ins.

Among the recorded examples of Doc Morrison's cracker-barrel philosophy are three rules for living which he passed on to Duke:

1, Always keep your word.

2, A gentleman never insults anyone intentionally.

3, Don't look for trouble but if you get into a fight, make sure you win it.

When I asked Duke if these were true, he roared with

laughter. 'Yeah, that's right. Except for the second one. A gentleman never insults anyone *un*intentionally. If you do it has to be for a good reason!'

Doc Morrison was a popular man who could never press his many friends for prompt payment of their bills so by the time Duke was six he was virtually insolvent. At the same time he developed severe lung congestion and started suffering from fits of coughing and spells of fatigue. His doctor told him to move to a warmer climate, warning that one more harsh Iowan winter might prove too much for him.

So in 1913 Doc sold his small business and went West alone, not looking for any rainbows or gold mines, just a good climate and the promise of opportunity where he could raise his family.

It was tough finding good land if you were a late arrival in those days but after weeks of searching Doc finally found a small ranch of eighty acres near Palmdale, California, on the edge of the arid Mojave desert. But it was land he could buy as a homestead over the years and he reckoned he could work it up.

Six months later Mary, Duke and his younger brother Bob trecked out too. The house was merely a glorified shack and the land was in miserable shape. But at least they had an air lift pump as good as any in the area which gave them some water for their crops, though not nearly enough.

They decided to grow corn and peas and by working together, sometimes fourteen hours a day, Doc and young Duke cleared sage brush and planted their crops.

'We were homesteaders in the real sense of the word,' Duke recalls. 'Rattlesnakes? We killed 'em by the hundreds. We just got used to them and they meant nothing to me as a kid, I saw so many. In the end, apart from not actually treading on them, we ignored them.

'But the jack rabbits were our real enemy. It's hard to believe the numbers of jack rabbits out there. We put some forty acres into corn while most other people were growing alfalfa and trying to raise cattle – which made it difficult enough. But we figured corn was our best bet as we couldn't afford any machinery.

'I remember my dad once planted five acres of black-eyed peas and we went out one morning and they were showing up nice

and green, about half an inch high. We went out again the
following day and there wasn't a piece of goddam green left.
The rabbits had cleared the lot in one night. Do you realize
how many rabbits that took?'

They were hard, rough days for his parents though to Duke,
a strong young boy who remembered little better, they were
merely adventurous. Not much of Doc's savings remained after
the first year, what with laying out for seed and basic implements,
making the initial payment on the farm and sending out for the
family. Not enough really to provide even the bare necessities.
Their staple foods were potatoes and beans, in one form or
another. It was a big day indeed when Mary served up frank-
furters once in a while.

And yet the Morrisons gained a strength from the soil they
tilled and by working hard, accepting misfortune with good
humour and pulling together, the family survived the first year
happily enough.

None of this harsh life destroyed Duke's natural curiosity or
his desire for knowledge. He went to school in the nearest big
town, Lancaster, some eight miles away, and to get there he
rode the family's old horse, Jenny, tethering her near the
school while he attended lessons.

Twice a week he picked up the family groceries from the
general store in Lancaster and strapped them across Jenny's
back along with his schoolbooks. The desert road was just caked
mud and sand meandering between the tall wind-hewn rocks.
On the days he picked up the supplies he'd sometimes be de-
layed until near dark but young Duke would enliven his home-
ward journey by playing games.

There was a big sharp bend in the road where it made a
turn around a cliff and he'd pretend a gang of outlaws were
waiting there to ambush him. He'd manage to scare himself
half to death, imagine he'd been pumped full of lead, then dig
his heels into Jenny and she'd gallop home.

By the time he ever did face outlaws it was some twenty years
later, *he* was the hero in the film and he always killed them
before they killed him.

Finally, however, Jenny caught a disease which made her get
thinner and thinner, no matter how much or what they fed
her. Outwardly the mare seemed to have nothing wrong with

17

her and at first the Morrisons couldn't understand it. Then some of the mothers in Lancaster, seeing how thin the horse had become, decided Duke couldn't be feeding her properly.

They began complaining to the local humane society who sent a representative to the school to talk to Duke. But Duke's teacher stood up for him. 'He feeds it oats every night and morning and waters it and does everything he's supposed to,' she told the man.

In the end Jenny was led away to a vet who diagnosed the disease and ordered her to be shot.

Jenny's death hit Duke hard. It was perhaps the first emotional tragedy of his young life and may partly explain why in all his western films he still insists on having only wranglers who love and care for the horses.

In any event, the Morrisons didn't have enough money to buy another horse so from then on Duke was picked up for school in a wagon.

After a couple of years, Doc Morrison had to admit defeat. Lack of money and the sterile Mojave desert had beaten him. That second spring their hopes had been high. Doc's health was better and after harvest time it appeared things might improve. But economically their second crop was a failure just like their first and the Morrisons now found themselves in almost desperate financial circumstances.

Mary ultimately convinced her husband that he just wasn't cut out for homesteading, especially against such heavy odds. After all, he had been a pharmacist not a farmer since the age of twenty and to keep fighting back against such a barren wilderness was, in her opinion, sheer folly.

So, their savings all but gone, the Morrisons moved out and down to Glendale, then a small town a few miles outside Los Angeles, where Doc went back to his old trade and worked in a pharmacy.

After two more years of hard work and scrupulous saving Doc once again acquired his own small drug store but with heavy payments to meet there was still no money to spare. By the time Duke was eleven years old he had his own newspaper round and was delivering prescripted medicines after school to provide his own spending money and to pay towards his clothes and upkeep.

The Morrisons lived next door to the local cinema and by delivering the theatre bills with his papers, Duke gained the additional perk of seeing all the movies free. They fascinated him. He loved the old cowboy stars like William S. Hart, Hoot Gibson, Tom Mix and Harry Carey. In his early films like *Red River* Duke worked with Carey and today Harry's son Dobie is a friend of Duke and appears in many of his films.

But Duke's favourite star in those days was Douglas Fairbanks senior. He admired his duelling, his stunts and agility, his fearlessness in the face of danger and his saucy grin when about to kiss the girl.

All the kids on Louise Street, Glendale, played at movies. They had actors, a director and a cameraman who used a cigar box with holes punched in it for a 'camera'. When it was Duke's turn to play leading man, it was Fairbanks he imitated, not the cowboy stars.

It was in Glendale too that he first got the nickname 'Duke'. (The well-told story that he was first called 'Duke' after reluctantly delivering a raw-boned caricature of a British Peer in a school play, is untrue.) He owned a large Airedale dog called Duke and on his way to Glendale High School he would leave the dog at the fire station and pick him up again on the way home. The firemen knew the dog's name but not his so they dubbed him 'Little Duke'. But when he started pushing six feet in height they soon dropped the 'Little'.

At this time one of the biggest trials of Duke's young life was having to shepherd his little brother Bob around. Wherever Duke went when he was out of school, Bob was sure to follow. Once when Duke was ten he was invited to a girl's birthday party. After the cake and ice cream had been consumed they began to play kissing games like 'Postman's Knock' but one boy suddenly pointed at Bob and said 'Get that little jerk out of here!'

Duke got angry at this insult to his brother, straightened the offender out in a junior style rough-house, only to lose the real victory because the girl's mother ordered him from the party.

To get his revenge, Duke fetched his air rifle, climbed onto the roof of the garage next door and shot down every balloon they had strung up in the party's backyard with beebee pellets. It was, Duke recalls, the first and last time he ever tried to redress a wrong with a gun in real life!

Despite his pre- and after-school errands, Duke still found time and energy to become a star football player for Glendale High and he became an honours student too. He ended up President of the Letterman Society, President of the senior class and a member of the debating team.

His graduation at Glendale proved to be an occasion of acute embarrassment. He had won the essay contest and his teacher told him part of his prize was that he could recite part of his essay to the whole school on graduation day. One line in the essay, which was about World War 1, went: 'And the worst thing the Germans had done was...' Every time his teacher had coached him he'd forgotten the word 'had' and on the big day he was very anxious to get the line right.

When Duke came to the difficult line he looked straight at his teacher and shouted 'And the worst thing the Germans *had* done was....' Then his mind went completely blank. All his attention had been on that one line and he couldn't remember a word that came after it.

Transfixed with embarrassment, he stood dumbly for a few seconds then bowed stiffly and walked off the platform. Years later when he visited his old school, people who had been present that day asked him what *was* the worst thing the Germans had done? He still couldn't remember!

During his last years at school Duke's ambition had been to join the US Naval Academy at Annapolis. But although he ended up fourth among thirty applicants, he was not selected.

Disappointed, he decided to capitalize on his great athletic prowess and entered the University of Southern California on a football scholarship in 1925. Again he had to work – to help put himself through university – and his first job was as a map plotter for the telephone company. He was paid sixty cents an hour for sitting in front of maps and charting where all the old lines and poles had been before they re-routed them.

When the phone company ran out of maps to plot, Duke had to find other ways of raising cash. One way he did it was to sell tickets to the USC football games to wealthy patrons. As a star player himself, Duke got two free tickets for every game but he wasn't likely to get very fat on the profits from just two so he bought tickets from other students too. He bought at ten dollars and sold them at fifteen – often to staff of an outfit called Muller Brothers, one of the biggest motor car agents in the area.

One day Duke took his tickets over to the Hollywood Athletic Club to see if he could get a higher price. It started to rain and as it was already Friday evening that looked like the end of *that* little enterprise. But the girl receptionist there told Duke 'Wait a bit longer, someone might still come in.'

Sure enough, in walked a chauffeur asking for tickets to the game. When Duke realized the man had been sent to get tickets or else, he thought what the heck, they're good seats. 'Sure,' he said 'I got a couple. Twenty-five bucks apiece.'

'That's a lot of money,' the chauffeur said. But Duke stuck to his guns. The chauffer went to call his bosses who finally okayed the price.

Years later the story had an amusing sequel. In the social circles of Newport Beach where Duke and Pilar now live they became good friends with the Muller Brothers who are co-directors of the Balboa Bay Club. Duke was regaling them with his tickets anecdote when their expressions made him stop. The chauffeur had been their own.

Most weeks during Duke's early university days his father would send him five dollars pocket money whenever he could afford it. But Doc was also a keen football fan so most weeks also Duke would send him a ticket for the game. Doc never knew up to the day of his death in 1938 that every time Duke sent him a ticket, he was losing himself around fifteen dollars in potential sales. And Duke, of course, never told him.

Around this time Doc got tired of the drug store business again so he sold it and opened an ice cream company. Duke recalls that he made the best ice cream he'd ever tasted, the kind you pay extra for. But Doc ran up against some pretty rough business methods from rivals. In those days refrigeration was out for small outfits, it was too expensive, so Doc bought his ice in blocks from a big plant and chopped it up so he could make his ice cream. Then a rival firm bought up all the ice in Glendale. They sold their produce to all the local drug stores, even gave ice cream away to people in the streets who promised to buy only theirs, and began to corner the market. Finally they verged on criminal monopoly by trying to buy up all the cream and milk in the area too and merging all the interests into one big company.

Ultimately Doc had to give in to these tough techniques and he went back into the drug store business again. All these failed ventures sapped his strength, but what really finished his working life was a severe electric shock.

As Duke himself remembers: 'He was up a ladder one day trying to sort out a fault with an electric cable and he got a terrible shock. We found him fallen on the floor. It affected him afterwards because one arm stayed numb from it. He just wasn't used to that kind of work.

'We weren't ever a wealthy or even comfortable family really but in small towns like Glendale it didn't matter that you didn't have a million dollars. It mattered more what you were as a person. And Doc was loved by most people as he always had time for everyone's troubles. And the kids all liked him.'

Right to the end Doc never lost his good humour nor his kindliness. There is no doubt Duke reveres the memory of his father and is grateful for the example he set. Although he saw his son launched as a successful actor, it is to Wayne's eternal regret that Doc died of a heart attack just a year before *Stagecoach,* the film that first put Duke on the road to international stardom in 1939. It is sadly ironic that Doc didn't live long enough after his hard life to see his son really launched on the career that has made him one of the all time greats.

During his summer vacations at university Duke had to find new ways of raising money so he approached his coach, Howard Jones, who sometimes procured well-situated boxes at the games for top actors. One day when Tom Mix, the top cowboy star of the day, asked for a good box, Jones said he would arrange it if Mix would help Duke Morrison and a co-footballer Don Williams to get summer jobs at the film studio. Mix agreed and a few days later he sent for Duke and Williams who were ushered into the star's dressing room on the old William Fox Studio lot.

Inside the luxury suite of the star who in those days was earning seventeen thousand dollars a week, Duke stared in awe at the photos round the walls: Tom Mix in Europe, Tom Mix in Africa, Tom Mix in one film after another.

Mix sat down, looked at the two husky young men before him and said 'Men, a star owes it to his public to keep in fine physical condition. Now I'm going to make a picture called *The Great K And A Train Robbery* in mid summer and I'll take you two boys along. You can be my trainers and we'll run two or three miles every morning. That will keep us all in good shape – you for football and me for the picture.'

But not right then because it was too early in the summer. So in the meantime Mix sent the two over to George Marshal, a director who was then head of the Fox lot, with instructions to find them work. Marshal gave them jobs as set dressers – moving furniture and props about the studio – at thirty-five dollars a week, the most Duke had ever earned up to that time.

One day Duke was told to report to an assistant director for John 'Jack' Ford, one of Hollywood's greatest directors, who was making an Irish picture called *Mother Machree*. Ford needed an extra prop man. In those days, before unions and ultra-specialisation, prop men had charge of all sorts of things – props, furniture, special effects and even some of the animals.

Ford had built a huge outdoor set of an Irish rural scene and to give it an authentic touch he had a large flock of geese there. Most of the time the geese weren't needed but *they* didn't know that and kept waddling under houses and under the specially built artificial mountain.

So Duke Wayne's first job on a John Ford picture was as a geese herder! Not that Duke minded one bit. He'd never been paid so much for doing so little.

During a break in shooting, Ford, a tough powerful man who brooked no arguments from his actors and took no nonsense from anyone, looked across at Duke and shouted 'Hey, goose-herder!'

Duke, easy-going, went over with a smile and Ford said 'So you're a footballer, eh? A guard?'

Duke nodded and said he was.

'Right, let's see you get down into position.'

Now Duke had had to put up with a lot of this kind of chaffing because right then the USC football team was the best they'd ever had on the west coast and Hollywood had gone wild about them. Nearly everywhere he went someone would say 'Show me how you get down in position.' And always Duke would think 'How in hell can I show them? I'm not busting into anyone!' But he'd get down on all fours, brace himself so they could pull and push him a little and let it go at that.

So when John Ford challenged him he thought 'Same old rubbish' and braced himself on all fours again to let Ford have his moment of fun.

But Ford had played ball himself and suddenly he lit out and kicked Duke's arms from under him so he went flat on his face in the plaster mud, in front of everyone. That made Duke really mad.

'Let's try it again,' he said quietly. Ford charged, went to dodge round him but Duke whirled and hit Ford right across the chest, dumping him heavily on his backside.

There was a deadly silence as Ford was highly respected, if not feared, and Duke thought 'Well, I've just charged my way out of the picture business.'

Ford sat there a moment in shocked surprise then threw back his head and roared with laughter. Then everyone on the set joined in. It was the start of one of the most profound friendships of Duke's life, a friendship which still endures today. In later years Ford and Duke together made some of the finest films Hollywood has ever turned out, like the classic western *Stagecoach, The Long Voyage Home, She Wore a Yellow Ribbon, They Were Expendable* and *The Quiet Man.*

From the moment Duke dumped him so spectacularly, Ford became aware of him. The awareness turned to liking and respect and whenever he could, Ford would get the young student work on a film, though at first it was only as a props man.

Mother Machree was significant also for being the starting point of Duke's close friendship with the late Victor McLaglen, its star. No one chortled louder than McLaglen when Duke dropped Ford. Today the Wayne–McLaglen relationship endures – between Duke and Victor's son Andrew, who directs many of Duke's films.

Duke made *The Big Trail* when he was twenty-two. It was his first really large featured role. Although the first of the 'big screen' films, it failed because it came out during the Depression and many cinemas could not afford the new equipment involved. But it launched Duke as an actor

Westward Ho was one of the many films Duke made for the old Republic Studios. After this film, Republic upgraded Duke's films and also lent him out to other studios

Stagecoach was the film that made Duke a star. Directed by his old friend John Ford, it was the classic western of 1939 and changed the whole style of future westerns. Ford refused to make it till he found a producer who would let him star the unkownn Wayne as the Ringo Kid

In *Sands of Iwo Jima* Duke gained his first Oscar nomination. He played a tough Marines Sergeant who was first loathed by his men but who eventually wins their respect

This is one of the few times you'll ever see Duke Wayne in a drawing room! But in *The Wake of the Red Witch* Duke as the tough sea captain, Captain Ralls, is still the rugged outdoor man, holding a protesting Gail Russell over his shoulder with contemptuous ease as he talks to Gig Young and Luther Adler

In *The Quiet Man*, Duke has a lot of trouble with Irish colleen Maureen O'Hara when he retires to Ireland after a life as a pugilist in America. She resists his advances and believes him to be a coward because he will not respond to the bullying of her brother, Victor McLaglen. Duke and McLagen finally come to blows. The fight goes up and down mountain slopes, across streams, in and out of pubs and is held by many to be the greatest screen fight of all time

2

ACTOR BY ACCIDENT

From the deck of a minesweeper in the heaving swell of the Pacific Ocean off Catalina Island in the summer of 1929, Jack Ford was shooting a difficult and dangerous scene for his submarine film *Men Without Women*.

Duke, who was working props, was operating a huge air pressure pipe which was blowing great globules of air up from deep in the water. Ford's idea was to get shots of men coming up in the air bubbles as if they'd been shot out of the escape hatch of a stricken submarine.

Everything was perfect for the shot: the sky, the clouds, the positions of the little shore boats, even the smoke from the boat's stack. In a few moments everything would change.

But the actors looked at the threshing sea, the other boats bobbing so close to them, and refused to dive in. They thought it too dangerous.

Ford, furious, glanced up at Duke on the upper deck and met his eye. He yelled 'Dook!'

'Yeah!' hollered Duke and did a spectacular dive overboard. He knew what Ford wanted – close camera shots of men's bodies catapulting to the surface – so he dived up and down in the air bubbles until Ford was satisfied.

That single action endeared Duke to Ford's artistic heart. He promoted him from third, to second and to first props man. This guy Duke Morrison was different, not like most of the other casuals, just hanging around to pick up a few fast dollars. He was ambitious, willing to learn and work and above all, he was thinking about *pictures;* not about his neck or special fees or time and a bloody half.

'The water *was* dangerous looking,' Duke recalls. 'But I had confidence those navy kids knew how to handle those shore boats, so I wasn't afraid of them running over me.'

On another occasion when filming a similar sequence, Ford wanted shots of men floating gently to the surface. The idea was a diver would go down, hang on to a heavy wheel until the camera was settled and then come up. Ford thought it would save time if *two* men went down, one to come up after the other.

They had one professional diver, so needed another man. Ford asked Duke to do it. Duke did some rapid figuring. He'd just lost a heavy bet on a USC game and was broke. The pro diver was getting seventy-five dollars per trip while Duke was getting thirty-five dollars a *week* propping.

'If I can get to do ten trips I'll make myself a clear seven hundred and fifty bucks,' he reckoned. 'That'll really set me up again.'

But just before he went in, Ford's assistant, an Irishman we'll call Flanagan, came up to Duke and said 'Sign this.' It was a *day* chit for seven fifty – seven dollars and fifty cents.

Duke glared at Flanagan but there was no time to argue. And Duke knew that Flanagan knew Duke would never go complaining to Ford.

Duke did the diving and to this very day he's certain Jack Ford doesn't know he only got seven dollars fifty cents for all that work. He wasn't *too* worried about it, however, for on the way back he played poker with the diver and managed to acquire a goodly share of the man's pay before they reached port.

But Duke swore to fix Flanagan.

Duke gained his first acting experience in bit parts in Ford films. First was *Hangman's House* in 1928, then his bit before the cameras in *Men Without Women*. In Ford's next, a film called *Salute*, about life at Annapolis Naval Academy (which Duke had wanted to join from school) Ford clapped Duke in a uniform and gave him a few lines.

It was on *Salute* also that Duke got even with Flanagan but more of that later.

For the film Ford wanted to hire the entire USC football team and take them to Annapolis. He had a liaison man who had made several visits to talk to the university authorities but didn't seem to be getting anywhere. In frustration Ford went to Duke for help.

Duke immediately thought of his coach, Howard Jones. He got Ford and Jones together but after some argy bargy with the authorities, Jones failed too. The main trouble was that Ford wanted the players out of school two weeks early, before the summer vacations.

Finally Ford went to Duke for the last time. 'Can you get me these guys or can't you?'

'Yes,' said Duke without hesitation. He didn't as yet know how.

'Well, get 'em,' said Ford. 'You can pay 'em each fifty to seventy-five bucks a week, no more. I'm going away so deal with Ryan, head of casting. But get 'em.'

Duke went straight to the head of the Scholarship Committee and talked like he'd never talked before. He convinced his superior that with a bit of extra work on the part of the professors not only would the boys complete their curriculums but would get good summer pay and would broaden their minds by going to Annapolis, visiting Washington D. C., the capital, see a bit of Philadelphia and also attend the top track meet of the National Collegiate Athletic Association of America.

Then he went to the students and to save his employer money he offered them a straight fifty dollars a week. Of course they jumped at the offer. Duke went back to Ryan and told him the team was all set. But just as he was leaving Ryan's office he had a sudden thought.

'Wait a minute,' he said to Ryan. 'I'm on salary here as a prop man at thirty-five bucks a week. Your liaison man who failed to fix this deal is on five hundred a week. What about me?'

Ryan thought a moment. 'Tell you what,' he said, 'I'll give you the same as the other kids. Fifty a week.'

As he left, Duke made an effort not to slam the door. 'Great,' he thought. 'I save the company a lot of dough by employing the boys at fifty a week instead of seventy-five and so wind up doing myself out of another twenty-five bucks a week. From this moment on I cease to be a company man!'

It was on *Salute* that Duke first really got to know another great lifetime friend, the late Ward Bond, who became so universally popular when he played the tough wagon-master Seth Adams in the *Wagon Train* TV series.

Bond turned up when Jack Ford was auditioning the footballers. He wasn't on the USC team at all but Ford took one glance at his rugged looks and said 'I want that big ugly guy too.'

Duke, who had another pal in mind for the job, said 'If it's a *real* ugly guy you want I've got a pal much uglier than him!'

But Ford wanted Bond. And when he was hired, Bond glowered at Duke and said 'Too bad, the passengers on your gravy train won't *all* be sweethearts!'

On the train Jack Ford's tough sense of humour came out. He put Duke and Ward Bond in the same berth. It started a friendship that lasted until Bond's tragic death from a heart attack in 1960.

It was mainly through Ward that Duke managed to get his own back on Flanagan. Ward had a few drinks on the train coming back and went into the dining car and ate a lunch costing eight dollars – in the days when four would have provided a really big lunch.

Flanagan immediately put all the husky hungry young footballers, destined to become *the* national football team of the year, on a ration allowance – giving them fifty cents less than what they could buy a reasonable meal for. They were really fed up.

Next morning Duke got them all together and said 'Let's go in and eat every damn thing we can and then sign the bastard's name on the checks.' So they did that – they ate ten to twelve dollar breakfasts and each signed Flanagan's name on his check.

When Flanagan went into the dining car to pick up the checks he started to rave. He tore up and down the train until he found Duke in the bar and yelled 'Duke, you're through!'

When the players heard about this all twenty-two of them trooped in and told Ford and his first assistant that Flanagan had fired Duke for playing this joke.

'Oh,' said Ford, 'Is that so?' Then they both went into the dining car, ate breakfasts as large as they could, and *also* signed Flanagan's name!

A sweet moment for Duke and it taught Flanagan a lesson for only paying him seven fifty for a seven hundred and fifty dollar job.

All this time Duke was only in the film world to get money to help him through university. He had drifted into acting by accident and he didn't as yet take it too seriously. One must remember these were the days when the film industry wasn't as structured or unionised as it is today. A keen young man like Duke could get to do almost any kind of work at all. He could work for four weeks as a propman and when that picture ended he could go to another studio for a week and work the lights. He could dress sets, work as an extra or help the wardrobe department. If someone was required to fall off a horse, Duke could do it. (He still can.) He did a great deal of stunt work in the early years.

As Duke points out, 'You could work in every department in those days, rather like in theatre repertory now. Then a man had his chance to find his place in the business. Today he would have to pay a thousand dollars in union fees, get into a dozen unions in order to do the things I did.'

But after *Salute* Duke's days at university were numbered. One day he and some friends went down to Balboa Beach to have a few drinks and to fool around at surfing. From afar off they saw a giant roller heading coastwards. None of the party wanted to tackle it so they dared Duke to do so. He pounded into the surf, did all right for a while but then the huge wave smashed him into the beach, tearing a ligament in his shoulder.

Out of footballing action for a time, he was valueless to Howard Jones so Duke went to work props again on a gangster film Ford was making.

One day he was carrying a table on his head across the Fox lot when director Raoul Walsh saw him. He watched Duke put the table down and walk back. He liked that slow, sure walk, the odd sort of shuffle with the cutting in of the hands across the body that still distinguishes Wayne's walk today. There was an honest, sincere, real look about the man.

'Who the hell is that?' he asked a crewman nearby.

'A guy called Morrison. He's at USC, a footballer.'

Walsh went across to Jack Ford and asked him about Duke. Ford's reply was wholly complimentary. At the time Walsh was putting together a two million dollar picture called *The Big Trail*. It was to be shot in the first big screen technique, the new 70 mm Grandeur process, and Walsh was looking for a good new leading man who wouldn't be too costly. At one time he'd been trying to get Gary Cooper for the role but 'Coop' didn't want it.

This was the period when motion pictures were changing to sound and all the New York stage actors and directors were flooding out west to Hollwood hoping to take over from the silent stars who had no voice technique.

Walsh had been testing all the stage actors sent to him but he was sick of their fancy walks, lift shoes, beards and loud gravelly voices.

After talking to Ford, Walsh went over to Duke and told him 'You're to stay on salary after this picture's over, then I want you to learn to throw tomahawks and knives and go to my dramatic teacher for coaching. I'm going to test you for the lead in *The Big Trail*.'

This is what happened after that, in Duke's own words:

'So I learned to throw the knives and tommyhawks. Then I went to this wonder coach from New York who was going to teach everyone how to act. Now I'd already seen this guy ruin a picture with Vic McLaglen and Myrna Loy. He made a hundred and fifty foot scene, all just talk, talk, talk, with all these beautiful words. This great director had been helping Ford out when he couldn't be there, and I'd seen just what he'd done. I didn't even want to go and prop for him if he could do that to Ford, so I had a dim view of him before I went to any of his private lessons. He was all very dramatic in his talk, all pseudo Shakespearean, and his idea of western dialogue was "GREETINGS GREAT BEAR, TELL THE GREAT WHITE MOUNTAIN HELLO FROM ME," all in great round vowels. He made me make sweeping gestures with my arms and mince up and down theatrically. I took about two weeks of that then I just quit going to him.'

Walsh went out one day to where Duke was throwing the knives and tomahawks and said 'You're doing great with this stuff but the drama guy tells me you haven't been going.'

Duke said 'If you want me to be that kind of actor, I can't cut the mustard.'

Walsh laughed. 'That's just what the guy said! He said you'd never make an actor in a hundred years.'

'Well, it's been fun,' said Duke. 'I'll go.'

But Walsh stopped him. 'No you won't,' he said. 'I'm testing you anyway.'

Duke's film test was almost catastrophic. He made it with

Tyrone Power Sr, one of the great Shakespearean actors of the day, and Marguerite Churchill and Ian Keith, both big stage names. They were standing on the set by a covered wagon.

Walsh told Duke, 'You're playing the leading scout of a wagon train heading west. There are no lines for you to learn. They'll just throw questions at you about the trip. Don't try to act. Just react naturally, as if it was happening in real life.'

But the actors *had* read the script. And they started hurling questions at Duke. How long is the trip? Where will we eat? Will we see any buffaloes? Will we be attacked by Indians? Duke started tripping over his own tongue and felt like a gauche, clumsy oaf.

He took it from the girl and from old man Power but when Keith started in on him, Duke got mad. Something he hadn't planned at all. He lost his temper and began hurling questions back at Keith.

'Don't say any more! Where you from, mister? Why you goin' west? Can you handle a rifle? You got pale hands, you sure as hell don't look the pioneering sort to me.'

Then Keith got confused and started to stammer and Duke thought this time he'd *really* blown it. He'd fixed Keith all right but himself too. But suddenly Walsh shouted out in delight.

'Cut! *He'll* do!' Duke had the role. Suddenly he was the star of a two million dollar spectacular. Star? His salary was all of seventy-five dollars a week.

But *The Big Trail* didn't exactly blaze any trails for Duke. It wasn't a bad picture at all but it was too far ahead of its time. An ironic fact too is that although it was Duke's first starring part, his first real chance, it is also the only film he's made in his career which lost money at the box office.

To show the film, all theatres had to do was buy a bigger screen and a 'squeeze' lens to fit on to their normal projectors to throw out the bigger image. It was a practical idea, certainly, but this was during the depression of the thirties and they couldn't afford the extra expense. Audiences could barely afford to go to the cinema at all in those times. As Duke puts it 'The poverty was incredible. They were breaking up boxes and building fires in the streets to keep warm, selling apples from their gardens for money. Ruined men were leaping from windows. '31 and '32 were very rough years and it was no time for fancy innovations in the movies.'

The cameras used to film *The Robe*, the 'new' big screen movie some twenty-five years later, were the same cameras that had been made for *The Big Trail*.

But one good thing did come out of the film. And that was Duke's screen name. Winfield Shehan, then production head of Fox studios, is the man generally credited for this. 'How can we have a star called Marion Morrison?' he argued with good reason. 'Marion sounds like the girl's name, Marian. Let's call him John Wayne.'

Duke made two more films under the Fox contract Walsh had signed him to, then they dropped him. Duke says one of the films, *Girls Demand Excitement*, may not have been the worst film he ever made but it was certainly the most embarrassing.

'All my friends were big healthy university kids and I worked in this picture where the dance director had me kissing girls up trees and while leaning out of college windows. For chrissakes, it was really embarrassing for a guy like me who should then have been playing in *the* national football team of the country!'

After one more picture like that, *Three Girls Lost*, Fox didn't pick up his option, the studio stopped his salary and let him go. But due to the publicity *The Big Trail* was attracting – mainly because of the revolutionary new process – John Wayne had become a minor 'name' and a week later he was on salary at Columbia studios.

Here he made one film, *Arizona*, then promptly fell foul of the studio's famous autocratic boss, the late Harry Cohn. A few weeks after Duke started at Columbia, Cohn heard rumours that Duke was drinking on set and fooling around with one of the girl stars.

One day Cohn called Duke into his office. He didn't mince words.

'Listen, I'm getting letters from people that you're drinking too much.'

Duke said 'What about it? I can't stop the letters, but it's not true.'

'Well, you just pay more attention to business around here,' said Cohn. 'And I don't want to catch you in any of the women's dressing rooms.'

It was obvious Cohn disbelieved Duke's strenuous denials because after that Duke found himself playing a small part 'heavy' in a football picture, standing in for a corpse in a scene in another picture, then nothing for six months.

Playing the corpse irked Wayne. It was in a film where Ian Keith was killed and he was supposed to lie on the ground throughout the scene. But Keith had to fly up to New York and instead of getting an extra, they made Duke put on his clothes and lie there in his place.

'I was a twenty-three year old kid,' Duke remembers. 'My dad had been a most wonderful man and because of him I naturally had a tremendous respect for older people and I'd never been treated like this before. The old son of a blank. But I did it. Today I would just have gone in and knocked him on his ear.'

After that Duke just twiddled his thumbs, drawing his salary without working for the next six months, then Columbia let him go.

Shortly afterwards Sid Rogell, a film boss who became a big wheel at Republic Pictures when Mascot Productions merged with Monogram, Consolidated and Lone Star Productions in 1935, called Duke on the phone.

'We've got a western series going and we want to talk to you. How do you feel about it?'

It was a series of B westerns but Duke recalled the advice given to him by the late Will Rogers: 'Don't worry what you're workin' in, just keep workin'.' He said he was interested.

A week later Rogell called him again. 'Duke, I have some bad news.'

'What is it?'

'Do you drink?'

'Well, certainly I drink.'

'Do you drink on sets?'

'Absolutely not.'

'Well,' said Rogell, 'I've got word you were drunk on sets, you were a rebel and wouldn't do what you were told to do, that you're just an all-around no good.'

'Where did you get this information?'

'Pretty high up in this business.'

Duke thought a moment then said 'Listen, you get that son

33

of a blank to say that in front of me and I'll kick his goddam teeth in.'

Rogell said he'd check his source again. Two days later he called Duke in and they signed the contract. The series did quite well but Duke found himself plugging along in quickie westerns and sage brush operas for some nine or ten years after that.

In 1933 Duke married Josephine Saenz, the beautiful dark-haired daughter of the Panamanian consul in Los Angeles, whom he'd first met surfing at Balboa beach during his university days. His career wasn't going too well at this time and Duke has been quoted in the past as saying 'I was in Hollywood's Poverty Row when I married Josephine and we first set up home in a small furnished apartment.'

'Poverty Row' may be a relative term for a film actor to use because clearly by normal standards he was doing quite well. But Duke was conscious that as an actor who had starred in a super epic, as a man who enjoyed the friendship of men as eminent as director Jack Ford, he could and perhaps ought to be doing a great deal better. When his first son Michael was born within the year, then Toni, his first daughter, followed by Patrick and finally second daughter Melinda, Duke became increasingly conscientious about providing a good living for his family.

In fact he was so anxious to give his children the best possible home and upbringing and at the same time to increase his stature as an actor, that he worked all his waking hours, heading for the studios at 6 am, arriving home dead tired at 10 pm, or else he'd be away on location for weeks at a time.

Paradoxically, but as in common with many Hollywood star marriages, personal bonds of love and companionship seem to bind stronger during the earlier years when a couple are facing comparative adversity together. Once the artiste – he or she – becomes a star name and faces all the attendant onslaughts of stardom, the demands on one's personal time, the approbation of one's peers, the rising of one's personal stock in a fast-moving creative milieu, it becomes too, too easy for the non-professional partner to cling to previous ways and standards, to be in fact left behind. It's not just a matter of a star's non-pro wife being left outside the circle at social functions while her husband becomes the cynosure of the group. He can always haul her in too if he really wants to. It's more the changes in their ways of thinking. The star has to keep up in a highly competitive cut-throat world which presents many problems, especially to a youngster. The partner receives no such challenges, nor the stimulations. While Duke was the least likely man to be personally affected by the enormous pressures of stardom, his marriage was eventually to prove no exception to the rule.

3

TOUGH, FINE EARLY YEARS

I've often felt annoyed when I've heard critics and others dismiss John Wayne as 'that cowboy star' or with phrases like 'that rootin', tootin', fast-shootin' son-of-a-gun hero by Hemingway out of Hollywood', and similar pat idiocies. Wayne has been an actor now for well over forty years. For thirty years he's been at the top. For the last twenty he's been the world's leading box office attraction more times than any other actor in history.

This sort of achievement was not founded on luck but on sheer unadulterated hard work. Wayne knows more about the physical side of picture making than almost any man alive. And there's no doubt that it was during those ten lean years when Duke languished in the obscurity of scores of B type quickies for Warner Bros, Republic and Lone Star Productions that he learnt the basics of his craft – the hard way.

Duke became the screen's first singing cowboy in a series called *Singing Sandy*. It wasn't Duke's rumbling baritone audiences heard on the screen, however, but the voice of a real cowboy actor called Smith Bellew. Duke felt strongly that his own voice shouldn't be heard beyond his bathroom door! But he tweaked the guitar and mouthed the words while Bellew supplied the noise.

After a few of these had been made, Duke felt so foolish, especially when fans on his public appearances asked him to sing, that he demanded they find someone else. His studio then turned to a then obscure western singer called Gene Autry – who didn't do too badly out of it considering he became a multi-millionaire from such an undistinguished beginning!

Sitting on a horse serenading the ladies – or the horse – was hardly Duke's scene. Nor was riding past a tree and plucking a handy guitar from its branches.

Budgets were tight on these six-day sage brush horse operas which went out under such corny titles as *Ride Him, Cowboy, Haunted Gold* and *The Big Stampede,* and Duke still nearly always had to do his own stunt work.

It was during these years that he met another of his lifelong friends – the colourful ex-rodeo rider turned stuntman and latterly top action director – Yakima Canutt.

Duke and Yak, who was an actor in those days, actually invented the bar room brawling technique of throwing murderous looking punches that do untold damage to thin air. The blow narrowly misses and the sound of the punch is added to the sound track later.

It wasn't that they were such great inventive geniuses. It was pure expediency. They raced through film after film with such speed that if they'd carried on the old system of screen fighting – where actors actually hit each other's shoulders – they'd have been eternally black and blue.

Duke remembers how he first met Yakima Canutt. 'It was on one of those western serials and we were in a rock quarry working till midnight. Our hours weren't our own in those days! The boss said "Okay boys, that's it. Be back in the quarry at four in the morning." Everyone groaned including Yak who said there were no buses and how in hell was he going to get home?'

'Eventually they let him take a company car. As he was leaving I got a fire going, a little Indian fire, and Yak yelled "Goddam it, this Duke guy reckons on staying here all night!" The upshot was Yak joined me and we swapped yarns till it was time to work again.'

One dangerous stunt Duke and Yak performed together was where Yak had to gallop down a steep hill on a horse, dive from his mount and 'bulldog' Duke off a moving railway handcart and roll on down the hill with him.

Something went wrong the first time they tried it and Yak came off his horse a shade too soon. As Duke roared, Yak shouted:

'All right, you son of a b . . ., what do you want to do? You want to come down off the horse and bulldog me? Okay, and I'll double for you.'

Now Yak was losing his hair back in those days so to nettle him further Duke said 'You'd better grease some colour into your hair if you're doubling me!'

They did the shot but Yak lost his hat. Nothing more was said at the time. It didn't matter much anyway as in those quickies who was to notice? But Yak had a plan in his mind to get his own back on Wayne. He got one of his girl fans back in Iowa to write him a letter. He showed it to Duke and it read:

'Dear Mr Canutt,

Why don't they make *you* the lead in those pictures instead of John Wayne? John Wayne's hat came off in that shot on the railway and I saw his bald head.'

Many in the film world believe Duke copied Yak's rolling walk and low quiet way of talking. But the truth is a little different. In the old days, to portray toughness actors pulled faces and growled at each other, Yak included.

One day Duke said 'No, Yak. I've seen you when you're *really* mad – and I *know* you're tough. It's a kind of smile and a straight way of looking at a guy and the voice drops low – when you're *really* being tough. So quit making those faces. I'm going to copy you when you really get mad.'

One of Duke's best stories about his days with Canutt concerns the time when both were making a film with a mean penny-pinching producer. Yak had to drive a Cadillac down a steep slope and a sharp bend, bounce it in front of the camera and drive on out. Just before he did it the producer leaped out and said 'You won't let this car get damaged, will you?'

Yak shouted 'Get out of my way. I'm the one who has to get out of this mess alive!'

Later at lunch with everyone sitting around, Yak was eating his sandwiches and drinking a little carton of milk, still half angry, when the producer looked over and said 'I didn't know tough guys drank milk.'

This was during the early days of the war and quick as lightning Yak glared at him and growled 'Hitler drinks a gallon of it every day!'

The same producer was such a cheapskate that on one movie he gave Noah Beery Jr a room without a bath. Beery made a fuss about it. Later when Yak and Beery were going to have a fight scene, the producer said to Yak 'Do me a favour, rough him up a little.'

Yak yelled 'What do you think I am for chrissakes. I'm over twenty-one! But you get him to call me the same things he called *you* and I'll kick the shit out of him!'

Duke can reminisce for hours about his experiences with Yakima Canutt. Certainly he's one of the best loved characters in the film world, if largely unknown to the public. Born in Colfax, Washington, on 29 November 1896, Canutt was World Champion All Round Cowboy in 1917, a title he held for seven more years. He was one of the greatest rodeo riders of all time. He made his film debut in 1924 but branched off into stunt work and character acting when talkies came in as he felt his voice was too high for a western hero. By 1937 he was king of the Hollywood stunt men and he established his own troupe of stunt boys and trained horses. It was Yak who staged most of the sensational chariot race in the 1959 version of *Ben Hur*.

Today he is past his mid seventies but is still an action director. And he and Duke keep regularly in touch.

No star today does the kind of stunt work Duke had to do in those early westerns and when Duke talks of some of the stuntmen he remembers and worked with there is respect in his voice.

'We had one guy who went off a high cliff about forty feet tall with two horses,' he told me once. 'The horses wouldn't jump so we all got behind them and shoved them off. The guy didn't tell us he couldn't swim because he needed the money for the stunt and when he hit the river he came up yelling "Help" and went down. Then he came up, said "Help" very weakly and went down again. Then the two horses came near him – and a horse in water will try to climb on anything – and one of them clambered on top of him. Finally a big raw-boned cowboy dived in and saved him. And do you know what the guy got for the stunt? Fifteen bucks!'

Duke also remembers a little skinny guy from somewhat later days called Slossie, who worked as a combination script boy, extra and atmosphere stunt man. When he wasn't feeding off-camera lines to actors or making continuity notes, Slossie would be hoisted up on a horse and told to mingle with the full time stunt men. In those days the bigger the band of rustlers, the better the movie looked.

'Slossie did fine for years till he got working on a movie where the heroine got thrown from her horse over a hundred and fifty foot cliff. All the regular stunt guys were too big to double the actress so Slossie said he'd do it.

'It was almost like sentencing himself to death. He didn't even know what protective padding to ask for or how to prepare the ground so as not to break every bone in his body. But what *we* didn't know was that he was worried sick because his six-year-old daughter needed an operation and he couldn't pay for it. He needed two hundred and thirty-five bucks and that's what he said he'd do the stunt for.

'Somehow it went off okay – in that he lived through it. Luckily, he hit first into some bushes and when he came to at the bottom of that ravine on Iverson's ranch, the doc was feeling round for broken bones and giving him pain killer.

'Slossie asked if all went okay. They said it had, so he got the doc to take him to a phone so he could ring his daughter's doctor to go ahead with the operation. But the guy said there were complications and a second operation costing around a hundred and twenty bucks would be needed.

'By then Slossie could hardly talk but he asked to see the producer. "If you need another take to make it real good, I'll do it again," he croaked. "And for only one-twenty."

'There were quite a few guys around then with Slossie's kind of guts, though.'

Guts yes, and an enormous roistering sense of fun too. In the mid thirties and early forties when Duke's career was really moving into high gear he attracted round himself a hedonistic bunch of live-for-today characters who worked hard and played even harder. Men like Ward Bond, who also did some of those Lone Star quickies with Duke – usually playing the bullying heavy – and men like Yakima Canutt and Grant Withers, another giant like Duke, and Johnny (Tarzan) Weismuller were all in the group.

Duke loved a spot of spirited horseplay with his drinking pals in those days and the group were fondly – sometimes not so fondly – known as Jack Ford's Rolling Stock Company. A phrase which needs no further elucidation. These big beefy guys frolicked so vigorously that the club house of the Hollywood

Athletic Club is said to have borne the scars for years. Duke and Ward are said to have spent one happy hour competing to see who could push his fist through the most wooden door panels. All cheerfully paid for by them, of course.

But towards the end of the thirties after years of playing the B western hero, Duke knew he was in a rut. Once he tried to give them up for a year because he felt they were losing him what following he had among western fans. But naturally enough he got scared. He had a wife and four children to support and he had an insecure feeling that if he stayed out too long no one would want him, not even for quickies. So when another contract was offered he took it, although it wasn't much better than the others. 'I've got responsibilities and I've got to keep working,' he said at the time.

In 1936 he went to Universal to make a string of cheap non-western action pictures. At the end of 1938 he returned to Republic to replace Bob Livingston in *The Three Mesquiteers* series. This boosted his image somewhat but it still wasn't the big kick he needed to get the top feature film roles.

But all the time Duke still had his valued friendship with director Jack Ford who now knew from Duke's showing in *The Big Trail* that he had real acting promise. All through the thirties Ford helped keep Duke's spirits up. 'Get all the experience you can, in anything you can get,' he'd tell his younger friend. 'Just keep getting plenty of screen time.'

One day in the mid thirties Duke was out on Jack Ford's yacht and both men were relaxing with a drink. Ford told Duke he'd just bought the screen rights of a terrific short story called *Stage to Lordsburg* by Ernest Haycox which had just appeared in *Colliers Magazine*. He told Duke the basic details.

'Sounds great,' said Duke who knew Haycox's work.

'Why don't you read it?' said Ford, tossing the story over.

Duke read it there and then and knew it would be a winner. It had all the classic Bret Hart type western characters in it and a strong story line.

They discussed it for a while, then Ford asked Duke 'Who the hell can I get to play the lead in it, would you think?'

Duke, who had just seen a fine screen performance by Lloyd Nolan, replied, 'Hell, I know the right guy – Lloyd Nolan'.

Ford groaned 'Oh, dern you Duke. Can't *you* do it?'

Duke nearly dropped his drink with surprise. And for nearly four years after that Duke says he went around with bated breath because Ford, who was determined to use Duke, couldn't find a producer who would also agree. Duke was afraid Ford might change his mind and actually approach Nolan or some other actor.

Every studio, distributor and financier Ford went to felt if they put out such a costly picture with John Wayne in it, the theatre next door would put one of his western quickies up against it. Also he wasn't really well enough known nor a sufficiently proven actor.

But Ford stuck to his belief in Duke until finally top producer Walter Wanger accepted Ford's condition that Duke would play the key role of the Ringo Kid, although Wanger wasn't really too keen on it either.

Once he'd got the go-ahead, Ford went to work – with all the painstaking care in writing, action, direction and production the usual western lacked. He signed top scriptwriter Dudley Nichols to adapt the short story into a full length screenplay.

Each role was ideally cast: Claire Trevor as the prostitute with a heart of gold, Thomas Mitchell as the drunken doctor whose pride is restored during a crisis. John Carradine as the outcast gambler who makes a last noble gesture. Louise Platt as the gentle southern woman who displays a will of iron. George Bancroft played the grizzled old Sheriff. Andy 'Gravel Throat' Devine played the zany stagecoach driver and Duke was the Ringo Kid, a young ruffian, good at heart, who when blamed for his father's death by shooting breaks out of jail to find the real criminals.

The film, finally called *Stagecoach,* was the great classic western of its time. It won three Academy Awards for 1939, revolutionized the whole western film genre and elevated Claire Trevor, Thomas Mitchell, John Carradine and Duke himself to stardom.

But Duke didn't know all this during the first few days of shooting. Jack Ford jumped all over him with both feet. He gave his young protégé the worst ragging of his entire career. Once he yelled at him. 'Don't you know how to walk? You're as clumsy as a hippo. And stop slurring your dialogue!'

In another scene Duke had nothing much to do but wash his

face and dry it, and Ford shouted 'Goddam it Duke, can't you wash your face properly? You look like a poached egg!'

He picked on Duke so much that Tim Holt, son of adventure film star Jack Holt, leaped up once saying 'Damn you Jack, quit picking on Duke like that.'

But Jack Ford was a clever man. He realized top seasoned actors like Mitchell, Carradine and Trevor might well resent a young unknown like Duke getting such a choice part and by giving him a hard time he put them on Duke's side. By taking the offensive against Duke, he could force the veterans to defend him. It worked too because one by one they came to Duke reassuringly and told him 'You're doing fine. Don't let that son of a b . . . get you down.'

Also, by bawling Duke out Ford could rouse his anger and thus help mobilize his emotions, making him give a better performance. He also wanted to help Duke shake off any bad acting habits he'd acquired in quickie westerns. Ford's tactics worked perfectly.

Duke subconsciously knew Ford must have a good reason for behaving as he did so he never complained. During one scene with Claire Trevor, however, he thought Ford had gone over the mark and he felt really angry. But Ford came up to him afterwards and apologized.

'I used you as my whipping boy in that scene,' he said 'because I wanted to get something special out of Claire. I couldn't yell at her but I wanted to get her up emotionally, so I yelled at you!'

Duke still remembers one example of Ford's tough sense of humour during the making of *Stagecoach*.

'He did play one really rough trick on me and it was lucky that I knew Andy Devine pretty well. After about three weeks of shooting Jack said "Would you like to see some of the picture?" I said "God, yes." He said "Right, you're not working for a couple of hours so we'll run a couple of reels through for you."

'Now, in my years as a prop man we'd done a lot of riding scenes and I'd figured out a way of getting reins to look natural when you're pulling them for a camera but there's no horse there. I used to put a spring arm exerciser at the other end to get a natural look to the action. So I'd told the prop man to be sure and get an exerciser for the reins when Andy had to pull on them. Of course he forgot and didn't do it.

'So I go and watch the two reels. When I came back Jack said "What do you think?"

'I said "A really terrific picture. It's the most exciting thing I've ever seen."

' "How do you like Mitchell?"

' "A terrific performance."

' "Claire?"

' "Great!"

' "Carradine?"

' "The greatest heavy I ever saw."

' "And what do you think about yourself?"

' "Well," I said, 'I'm playing *you*. I was just putty for you. That's the part of the picture most people will identify with and it's you. Naturally, for a director that's all I am – putty."

'Ford said "It's great of you to say that but have you nothing *constructive* to say about the picture at all?"

'I thought hard for a moment and said "Yes, about those reins Andy's supposed to be pulling on . . . I told that son of a blank prop man to get an exerciser . . ."

' "Hold it!" Ford yelled. "Right, I want everyone down here on the floor!" And he got them all down, the electricians from the lights, the prop men, the wardrobe people, all the actors and said "I want you all to know our new star John Wayne thinks the picture's great, that we're all doing a hell of a job. But he can't stand Devine's performance."

'I just stood there flushing. What in hell could I say? But Andy winked at me. He knew Jack's tricks.

'I didn't mind any of this too much. When Jack stopped doing that sort of thing you were no longer his man. If he didn't like you, you just weren't there, you didn't even exist.'

Duke also knew *Stagecoach* was the big chance of his life and he took his work on it extremely seriously. He rehearsed his scenes in front of a mirror at home and rearranged furniture in his room to match the set-up of next day's shooting and worked out every move so he'd know exactly what to do when the cameras rolled.

One day the film's producer Walter Wanger walked on to the set and to his horror saw Wayne clamber on the roof of a careening, rolling stagecoach. He shouted at Ford to get his new star down from his dangerous perch. 'Hell,' said Duke later. 'He didn't know I'd been doing that kind of stunt for years just for eatin' money!'

Stagecoach was the hit film of the year and Duke's career really began to move for the first time – more than ten years after he'd first started to act. Most studios now wanted him to star in their big budget pictures. At one time in the forties Duke had nine films on first run release. No other actor in the world has been able to claim that.

It was no wonder that for the next twenty years or so whenever Jack Ford wanted Duke for a picture, the only question Duke asked was 'What hat, which door and when do I come in?' There never has been a written contract between them. It wasn't only loyalty to the man who'd given him the breaks but also because he knew any film Ford made would be a fine, probably even a great one.

This doesn't mean Duke ever stood in awe of Ford, although he revered the older man. In fact, when Ford, Duke and Victor McLaglen were making *The Quiet Man* in Ireland years later, word arrived that Ford had been appointed a Rear Admiral in the US Naval Reserve. Duke congratulated his old friend by pushing him off the pier into Galway Bay.

They are still great friends of course. When Duke cracked a couple of ribs while filming *The Undefeated,* Ford sent him a telegram: 'Dear Duke, what's new?'

4

NO 'ANTI'
BEFORE THE HERO

Once Duke's career switched into top gear it never really changed down again. The Ringo Kid was ideally suited to his admitted limitations as an actor at the time and his screen persona for the next decade developed indirectly from it.

A young rugged giant of few words, he was hard with men but shy with girls. His face was the great American face – tough, friendly but completely masculine. It showed great individual strength plus an attentive simplicity and sincerity towards his friends. He didn't underestimate his opponents but respected their strength and courage. He never made a film of salacious sex or played a part which glorified the psychotic weakling. Anti-heroes were not for him. Most of the movies had pace, humour and lusty clean sex, if any. Violent and romantic by turns, Wayne had an air of complete invincibility and he dealt only with basic emotions. He identified with something real in the characters he played and sold sincerity all the way down the line. He was nearly always the rugged champion who helped the underdog and who served the cause of justice single-handed if he had to.

But Wayne's appeal had more than mere physical attraction or simplicity. It came from his emotional strength which in turn came from his own pioneer heritage, as American as most of his pictures. These, over the next two decades, tended to glorify the eternal physical and emotional verities which most people believe make life finer – friendship, loyalty, integrity, love and the eventual triumph of good over evil.

To millions of filmgoers in whose private lives good and evil often waged dreary and inconclusive battles, John Wayne's constant portrayal of the triumph of good was not only good entertainment but personally reassuring.

In recent years his screen character has broadened and has taken on once undreamt-of dimensions but most of the early ingredients are still there.

After *Stagecoach* Duke made *Allegheny Uprising,* a mild success, and in Raoul Walsh's *Dark Command* in 1940 he gave a competent performance as a Texas Marshal quelling Quantrill's Raiders after the American Civil War.

Then, as if to remove any lingering doubts that maybe Duke's performance in *Stagecoach* was a mere flash in the pan or that he was only good for western roles, Ford had Duke play the good-natured, inarticulate homesick young Swedish sailor Ole Olson in Eugene O'Neill's *The Long Voyage Home*. It was one of the best films of 1940 and Duke made a convincing Swede, more than holding his own among some of Hollywood's finest character actors.

He indulged in some naval heroics with Marlene Dietrich in *Seven Sinners,* then made a rather unsuccessful stab at light comedy in *Lady For A Night* in 1941. Cecil B. de Mille cast him as the unstable but honest sea dog Captain Jack Martin in his epic sea drama *Reap The Wild Wind* the following year.

In Henry Hathaway's western *Shepherd Of The Hills,* Duke's laconic dialogue and rolling walk were still there but his acting was acquiring more maturity. In the mid forties he made several good and a few run of the mill horse operas and adventure films, most of which were routine 'star' roles which helped along his heroic image. There were popular westerns like *The Spoilers,* William McGann's *In Old California* and *In Old Oklahoma,* where Duke played a cowboy fighting off the Indians for the oil barons.

In *Flying Tigers* in 1942 Duke hit upon another ideal showcase for his big star personality – the war film. In *The Fighting Seabees* in 1944 he consolidated this formula and like many top stars in those days his war films naturally contained large doses of propaganda to back up the morale of America's fighting men abroad, not to mention the spirits of the folk back home as well. He made *Tall In The Saddle* in 1944 and worked with his old friend Ward Bond in *Flame Of The Barbary Coast* the same year.

47

There is no doubt Wayne was now the hardest worked star actor in Hollywood. He had been trapped in those low-budget quickie westerns for so long that now, with a family of four children to support, he worked like a demon. For several years he made one picture after another with never more than a week's rest between them.

Working as hard as he was it seemed inevitable that something had to go. Unfortunately it was the marriage to his first wife Josephine Saenz.

Of course a marriage doesn't break up purely because a man is working hard but personal differences between Duke and Josephine had begun to emerge. She was never particularly fond of his 'Rolling Stock Company' buddies, nor the fact that Duke and his pals liked to have a drink upon the odd occasion and to kick up boisterous, if innocent, hell now and again. Duke was never a tuxedo man yet Josephine preferred the quieter more elegant Pasadena society parties.

Duke has never expressed anything but praise for Josephine as a wife and mother. At the time of their separation in 1942 he was reported as saying 'I didn't really ever do anything wrong, except stay away from home too long maybe. I was working so damn hard and I thought I was doing the right thing then. Jo and I just difted apart. She's a fine girl and a really wonderful mother.'

Duke had always been a loving and solicitous father and right from the time his career began to flourish, he set up trust funds for Michael, Toni, Patrick and Melinda. Everything he made out of merchandizing, for instance, went into the trusts for them.

Even after their divorce in 1944, when Josephine received a reported settlement of seventy-five thousand dollars plus a thousand a month alimony – which went up to two and three thousand a month as the children grew older – Duke regularly visited his children who, as is usual in California law, had been given into his wife's custody.

Within six months of the divorce Duke and Josephine were back on friendly terms and they cared about the children together, with Duke sharing the worry over things like braces for Melinda's teeth, glasses for Toni, and over all their youthful ills, like tonsil operations.

In *The Conqueror*, Duke played Ghengis Khan complete with droopy moustache and eyes slanted by special make-up. The public showed their displeasure at this departure from Duke's normal outdoor roles and stayed away in droves

In *The Searchers*, Duke played Ethan Edwards, a harsh and unbending man who returns from a hunt for cattle rustlers to find his brother's family wiped out by Indians. His search for the killers becomes a personal vendetta and Duke conveys something of Edward's tragic loneliness

As Duke told me himself 'Josephine was always such a wonderful mother. I and the kids owe her a great deal.'

In Hollywood where more than eighty per cent of actors' marriages founder in divorce, it is easy to find the maladjusted children of the top film names. Newspaper files are liberally sprinkled with reported cases of their misdeeds, some tragic, many self-indulgent.

The fact that none of Duke Wayne's children have ever given him cause to feel anything but pride speaks for itself. All his four children by his first marriage are themselves married with large families of their own. And when Duke and his wife Pilar, together with *their* three children – Aissa, Ethan and Marisa – hold 'open house' it is indeed a family sight to behold. More than enough for *two* football teams get together on Duke and Pilar's beautiful green lawns at Newport Beach. His first four children have now given him no fewer than sixteen grand-children – and in the midst of them all there stands Duke with a big boyish grin on his face, looking every inch the beloved patriarch he is.

During World War II Duke was well into his thirties and when he was rejected for service he was anything but pleased. But the fact remains that in films like *They Were Expendable*, a Jack Ford semi-documentary picture about the small high-powered torpedo patrol boats in the first frantic days of America's entry into the war in the south Pacific, Duke could do more for his country and fighting men's morale than he could have done in the front line himself, just one GI with a rifle.

But Duke wasn't satisfied making films about war. He wanted to be out there himself, to go personally and do what he could for the boys fighting the war.

In 1944 he went. He spent three months taking camp shows round the Pacific war fronts. He performed as near to the action as he was permitted to get – in mangrove swamps and in kumi grass sometimes twenty-five feet high. And when he got back to America he launched into no rhetorical eulogies about heroics. He told it like it was.

'What the guys out there need,' he said 'are more letters, cigars, snapshots, phonograph needles and radios. And, if you can spare 'em, cigarette lighters. I can't say it strongly enough. Those guys are in a hell of a war. It's not only fighting but work

D

and sweat. They're where 130 degrees is a cool day, where they scrape flies off, where matches melt in their pockets and Jap 'daisy cutter' bombs take legs off at the hip. They'll build stages out of old crates, then sit in the mud and rain for three hours, waiting for someone like me to say "Hello Joe." We've *got* to do more for 'em.'

Duke worked from dawn till midnight and past, visiting every hospital he could find, and did his best to meet every wounded man in them. He didn't mention any of that though.

It's probable that Wayne's sense of super patriotism began in the war years. He has frequently been derided for his hawkish attitudes but in stars like Wayne and Bob Hope, America's fighting men have long known they have moral support. When Duke made *The Green Berets* in 1967 – to show his country just what the boys in the US Special Forces were going through in Vietnam – it was only an extension of the kind of work he has been doing for more than twenty-five years.

In Duke's next film *Dakota* he was teamed up again with Ward Bond. It was a good western where Wayne battled with range baron Bond (a villain yet again) to get land for the 'iron horse'.

It was about this time that Duke and Ward took some time off and went away on their famous hunting trip to shoot rabbits and quail near Hemet, California. They were all spread out and walking down a great step of grassy land when someone on Duke's right put up a rabbit. It ran across in front of Duke who said 'Goddam, I'll get it.' He took a shot and the rabbit went down. Suddenly there was a moan, then a series of more moans, and Ward got up out of the long grass holding his back and neck.

How Ward had managed to get there no one knew because he was supposed to have gone the other way entirely. But Duke picked him up and they rushed him to a country doctor who started digging around in Ward's back and talking of lead poisoning. They bundled Ward into a car and rushed him to another doctor in the nearest town who extracted some forty-two pellets from his back and neck, including one shot from his ear, which could have been dangerous. The pellets had gone right through a shirt, a hunting jacket and a canvas bag.

When Ward demanded to know why Duke had shot him,

Duke drawled 'Waal, I always wanted to see the pattern the shots made, just wanted to check they didn't spread out too far.' And Ward laughed louder than anyone.

In the early forties a group of actors went down to Mexico with hopes of buying a studio and setting up their own independent film company. Wayne, Ward Bond, Fred MacMurray and Ray Milland were among them. The studio never materialized but it was at a party down there that Duke met the girl who was to become his second wife, Mexican actress Esperanza Baur, a tempestuous and talented woman whose nickname was 'Chata'. (It meant Pugnose.)

Esperanza, a diplomat's daughter, had starred in the Mexican version of *The Count Of Monte Cristo* and was Mexico's second top actress. Duke saw her a good deal after his separation from Josephine Saenz. She came to Hollywood and was put under contract by Republic but she never actually made a film for them.

In January 1946 Duke and Miss Baur were married, with Ward Bond acting as best man. In 'Chata' Duke had a volatile companion who liked to drink and socialize along with himself and his pals and physically their union was a happy one, though she was unable to have children.

But the marriage was stormy from the start. Duke himself was quoted as saying 'Our marriage was like shaking two volatile chemicals in a jar.'

Right from the beginning Chata insisted her mother came to live with them. Although Duke had a relatively small house at the time, his den was converted into a bedroom for Mama. Duke would stay away on locations and when he got back he'd find the two women had virtually taken over the house.

Over the next few years there were frequent rows and separations, with Mama moving back to Mexico City, Chata going down to visit her and staying away for months at a time, and Duke going down to persuade his wife to return.

Finally they bought a larger house and when they moved in after getting back from locations in Ireland for *The Quiet Man*, Mama moved back too. From then on the situation deteriorated.

Duke's four children made their film debut in *The Quiet Man* and spent some time with Duke and Chata in Ireland. Chata was always rather uneasy about Duke's devotion to his children by his first marriage and she was never very happy when they came to stay at the house.

The marriage ended in a stormy divorce suit in 1953. At first to newspaper reporters Duke said he felt it was his fault because he had been so busy working but finally, as her complaints against him were listed and published, he got angry. 'I refuse to be a doormat any longer,' he said.

In fact he got his suit in first, charging his wife with thirty-one specific cases of cruelty. Chata charged him on twenty-one counts. But in October 1953 the divorce hearing, which looked like becoming one of the most sensational in Hollywood history, fizzled out when Chata signed a relinquishment claim to their Encino home, a home in Van Nuys in which Duke was then living, and some oilwell properties, for an undisclosed settlement from Duke. Each was granted a divorce from the other.

Throughout it all, Duke preserved his dignity and good humour.

'What I dislike most is talking about her,' he was reported as saying at the time. 'It doesn't seem right but there's nothing else I can do now. There has been a lot of mudslinging from her side and a guy has to protect himself some time.' He was upset about the effect the testimony might have had upon his four children.

'There are things that happen in the life of every man and woman, things they aren't ashamed of, but events and feelings that aren't meant to be known by everyone in the world,' he said with truth. 'It just makes you a little sick to see them in black and white. I'm not cynical about women yet, but they are a little lower on that pedestal. Maybe the worst part of it is that everyone will think there were no good times or love during our marriage. But there were.'

It was during the early days of his marriage to Esperanza that Duke decided his acting was becoming predictable – he was being too much the big unassailable hero. So in 1946 he had another go at light comedy – co-starring with Claudette Colbert in Mervyn Le Roy's *Without Reservations*. Miss Colbert played a woman novelist who wanted to star Duke, an ex-Marines Captain, in the film of her book. It wasn't a huge success but at least Duke proved he could handle comedy better than he had in *Lady For A Night*.

It was in 1947 that Duke took a step which years later was to be copied by many major actors – he became a producer. There were two very good reasons for this. First, he would have more control over his own work and the kind of roles he would play. Secondly, and somewhat more pragmatically, he could divert some of his income into the costs of making his own films and thus keep it from the extended fingers of the tax man.

Right from the time he made *Stagecoach*, he'd felt dissatisfied about the production bosses above him. He felt his judgement was as good as, if not better than, theirs. He told me the following story which illustrates the point:

'I was under contract to Republic when I made *Stagecoach* for U.A. but the guys at Republic, the jerks, just couldn't see how important it was to *them* to let me do it. In fact, they almost lost it for me. But when *Stagecoach* was finished I was asked if I wanted tickets to a special preview being held at the Westwood Theatre on the the UCLA campus. I said yes and I gave them to some executives at Republic and went to see it myself.

'Well, the audience just went crazy. It was a great film, anyone could see that. Next day I heard nothing from my studio. The following day I heard nothing. On the next day I went into the production office and to my boss and said "I saw you fellows at the film the other night but I've heard nothing from you, not a kiss my backside, not a hello, nothing. What's the matter?"

'They said "Well Duke, after we saw it we all went out and had a coffee and we decided if they want to make westerns they'd better let Republic make them."

'That film won three Oscars, changed the whole style of westerns for ever, elevated its actors to stardom including me, *their* property, and yet they could not see it. That's why an actor gets restless!'

But by 1947 Duke himself was the biggest property Republic owned and when he said he wanted to be a producer, strings were pulled and the big executive desk and office were soon provided.

'Making films is like painting a picture,' he said at the time. 'If you're having a portrait painted you wouldn't have one man do your eyes, another your nose and still a third your mouth. And that's what often happens in the movie business.

53

Instead of harmony in the final product you get a mixture, or even distortion. That's why I think production control should be centred in one man. I'm analytical because I played in so many bad pictures and I look for the things that can hurt actors. I'm lucky to have survived dozens of B pictures I made – they killed off many fine actors.'

His first co-production was *The Angel And The Badman,* a pacifist story strangely enough which Duke personally liked. It did fairly well.

In *Fort Apache,* for Jack Ford again, Duke turned in one of his best performances so far. In the story a martinet Colonel (Henry Fonda) takes over an Arizona fort refusing to heed his aide's knowledge of Indian fighting – with disastrous results. Duke's interpretation of the frustrated Captain Kirby York proved he'd now matured into more than the stereotyped American hero critics mostly took him for.

In Howard Hawks' epic western *Red River,* Duke endowed the ageing cattleman Tom Dunson with dignified authority. *Red River* was also notable as being the film in which he first obtained his famous old Cavalry hat.

Now this hat has quite a story. It turned up among the props and Duke immediately 'liberated' it. He'd always wanted a hat that looked as old as the one Jack Ford wore and here it was, at least thirty years old. He wore it all through the picture and on his next, *Three Godfathers,* which Ford directed. In the middle of this picture a dust storm snatched the hat from Duke's head and sent it whirling across the desert. The cast and crew, spent an hour searching for it in the twilight. However, hat or no hat, Duke delivered a finely tuned touching performance as one of three bank robbers who risk their lives to rescue a new-born baby in the desert.

His hat, which became a sort of good luck mascot, was to figure dramatically in other incidents over the years.

In *Tycoon* and *Wake Of The Red Witch,* which Duke also co-produced, his performances were more routine. But by now he had been voted the world's most popular star at the box office – a position he still holds more than twenty years later. An astonishing fact is that way back in 1948 Hollywood trade paper columnists were writing phrases like 'Wayne has been at it for twenty years now and he's still at the top. What gives?'

Wayne became a fully-fledged producer in 1948 when he both produced and starred in *The Fighting Kentuckian* for Republic, a tough frontier story. In it Wayne made minor movie history by hiring comedian Oliver Hardy to play a feature role, one of his rare appearances without Stan Laurel.

At the end of 1949 and in early 1950 Duke appeared in two films which sent his stock and reputation as an actor soaring high. The first was *She Wore A Yellow Ribbon,* one of Jack Ford's classic movies which gave Duke one of his favourite roles. Again he gave a sensitive performance as an ageing man – an American Cavalry Officer who has to try and defeat Indians who were amassing for General Custer's last stand and so avoid a major Indian war. For this film Duke was in the running for an Oscar nomination. Strangely enough it was in the next film, *Sands Of Iwo Jima,* that Duke did win his first and only Oscar nomination – until he actually won the 1970 Oscar for *True Grit. Iwo Jima* was about young marines in battle during World War II. As the tough Sergeant Stryker who is at first loathed by his men and then wins their friendship and respect, Wayne gave a memorable performance.

It was during this period that one could see the pattern emerging of the unusually mature sexual involvements Wayne has with all his screen wives. In Ford's *Rio Grande,* the third in the great director's trilogy about the US Cavalry, Duke played another ageing man who loses his wife (Maureen O'Hara) and children's love in his ambitious climb for promotion but wins it back during the Apache wars along the Mexican border. A performance praised by the critics.

It was in *Rio Grande* too that Duke once again nearly lost his precious Cavalry hat. He was wearing it while fording a raging river when it fell in and got washed away and carried a full mile downstream. Finally crewmen in a boat retrieved it. With Duke yelling frantic instructions from the shore.

It was in 1950 that Duke finally left his exclusive contract with Republic studios and went over to Warner Brothers. His deal there was for one picture a year for seven years at a negotiable salary, plus ten per cent of the gross of each film. He could produce within their walls but for his own company. It was the first deal of its kind for any star.

The money and the offer of control were only part of the

reason he left Republic. He was also annoyed because they kept wavering about letting him make *The Alamo*, a film which even then had become the big ambition of his life. (In fact he didn't make it till ten years later.)

This is the story as Duke told it to me:

'I was all set to make *The Alamo* in Panama where I'd spent weeks scouting locations. There was a perfect area just outside Panama City which looked like the San Antonio area in Texas of the time. Panama was having a depression right then which would have made the whole operation cheaper. Also, there was a two mile airstrip nearby which the Americans had built so transport would have been easy.

'Just as I was all set to go, Herbert Yates, my boss, got chicken at the last minute. I said "You go through with this, Herb, or I won't be on the set when you get back." We were pretty good friends. He said "Well, I'll have to figure it all out again." I said "Come on, I've done plenty of favours for you. I've done all the figuring that has to be done, the locations are set up, we're sending men out there and suddenly you stop them."

'Well, he scratched his head and said "We'll talk about it again when I get back in two weeks." I said "I want the okay now or I won't be here when you get back." He said "Ha ha."

'As soon as he'd gone I called a moving van and took all my stuff out of the studio. And I never went back. It sure shook Herb but that picture had been a dream of mine for years and I was determined to make it. I felt he was belittling my efforts, besides refusing to do it. If he had said "Look, we don't have the money but it's a great idea" maybe I would have stayed but his attitude was such ... well, I left.'

Under his deal with Warner Brothers Duke made ten pictures in the fifties for his own company, which in 1954 he re-formed and called Batjac Productions. Among them were films like *The Bullfighter And The Lady*, *Operation Pacific*, *Big Jim McLain*, *Blood Alley*, *Hondo* and *The High And The Mighty*. But Duke made many other films for other studios besides, sometimes totalling as many as four a year.

In *Operation Pacific* with Patricia Neal Duke played a submarine commander who returns to his estranged wife after he'd deserted her following the death of their only child. He had a mature and unsentimental relationship with Janis Carter in

Flying Leathernecks and another with Maureen O'Hara in Ford's Irish comedy, *The Quiet Man*.

At about this time Duke decided to try to cut his own screen appearances from three or four a year to only two, so he could concentrate more on production. He wasn't getting any younger, he felt, and he needed to be more protected than to have all his eggs in one basket and leave them there. At the time he wanted to be sure when his acting days were over that he had made the rare transition from star actor to top-flight producer and director.

The Angel And The Badman, The Fighting Kentuckian and an excellent drama of the bull ring called *The Bullfighter And The Lady* – which he produced with Robert Stack, Joy Page and Gilbert Roland in the cast – were all successful enough to encourage him to go the whole hog and produce pictures *without* himself as the star.

But it proved to be more difficult than he'd thought.

Hondo for instance was meant to star Glenn Ford with whom Duke's company had a two-picture deal. But Ford didn't want to work again with Hondo's director so Duke had to solve the problem somehow. 'I found the story,' he said in the end. 'I like it, so *I'll* do it.'

In *The High And The Mighty* he had Spencer Tracy in mind to play the dependable, middle-aged pilot of the doomed airliner, but Tracy didn't want to do it. So Duke stepped into the breach again.

When *Blood Alley* began shooting, Robert Mitchum had been signed for the lead. Duke had even given him a third interest in the picture. Duke was on a much-needed holiday when he got a call from his producer William Wellman (who had helped Mitchum become a star with *The Story Of GI Joe*) who told him he was having big differences of opinion with Mitchum.

'Oh, he'll be all right,' laughed Duke. 'He's just been vacationing too long!'

But the differences were irreconcilable and Mitchum left. Wellman told Duke 'We can't get anyone else. The only guy who'd be any good is Humphrey Bogart but he wants. half a million dollars.'

No one was getting that kind of money in pictures then but Duke Wayne himself and when Wellman said he'd just have to come back, Duke abandoned his holiday and found himself yet again playing a role he hadn't wanted.

The odd thing is that both *Hondo* and *The High And The Mighty* turned out to be way above any films Duke as an actor had appeared in since *Rio Grande*. *Big Jim McLain,* made in 1952, had been dismissed by critics as blatant anti-Red propaganda. He'd done little but exercise stock mannerisms in a comedy *Trouble Along The Way* in 1953 and his other film that year, *Island In The Sky,* was a routine melodrama.

In *Hondo,* which was directed by the late John Farrow, Mia Farrow's father, Duke played a daring cavalry scout who risked his life to rescue a woman and her young son from Indians. His portrayal was a delicately blended mixture of toughness and sincere humanity.

And it was in *Hondo* that Duke for the third time nearly lost his beloved mascot, his Cavalry hat. It just disappeared from the location camp in Mexico and hours of searching failed to find it. Finally Duke asked a local radio station to broadcast its loss.

Three hours passed before a local peon with his six-years-old son arrived at the camp with the hat. The peasant sheepishly admitted his son had wandered into the camp when the crew were away shooting, had seen the hat and reasoned that surely such an old hat must have been abandoned by the rich Americanos, and had taken it. But when they heard on the radio that it was the hat of John Wayne, a very good friend of Mexico, they hastened to return it. Duke sent him off with pockets full of pesos.

Duke's next film was also with John Farrow, a slow moving drama called *The Sea Chase*. In it Duke played an anti-Nazi German sea captain, a strange piece of miscasting, and almost to a man the critics dismissed his performance as unconvincing.

I doubt if there was any connection at all, but at the time Duke was making the film, in a superb location in Hawaii, he had fallen deeply in love with the beautiful Peruvian actress Pilar Palette.

Pilar went with Duke, chaperoned by his secretary, and towards the end of the film Duke was hoping his divorce decree would become final in time so that he could marry Pilar in a gorgeous Hawaiian setting.

And it did. It came through on their last day there.

5

PILAR

The first meeting between Duke and Pilar Palette, his future wife, certainly had an odd setting. It took place in a South American jungle near Tingo Maria in Peru.

Duke was in Peru scouting locations for his long-planned film *The Alamo,* having abandoned the idea of making it in Panama. Based temporarily in Lima, Duke was one day invited to visit the jungle location of a Peruvian film.

Partly out of courtesy, partly to see if the spot might be usable in his own picture, Duke decided to go.

Long before he was introduced to Pilar, who was one of the stars of the film, Duke had become aware of her. As Pilar stood demurely waiting her turn to be introduced, Duke's eyes took in her thick black hair, pale skin, huge dark liquid eyes and her lithe slender figure. She had an air of unusual grace and elegance about her.

Pilar herself, who like everyone else in the unit had known of the big American star's visit to their location, was not the kind of girl to be unduly impressed by movie stars. Her father had been a Senator in the Peruvian government for twenty-five years, all her life she had travelled constantly with her family and her upbringing had been sophisticated.

As a child in Lima she had seen many American films of course, but her favourite star in her young days had been Gary Cooper. Shortly after she became an actress, however, Pilar saw Duke in *Tycoon* and if she had been pressed at the time to name her favourite star, it would have been a toss-up between Duke and 'Coop'.

What first impressed Pilar about Duke as a man was his height – he simply towered over everyone else – and his air of confident, quiet authority. She liked too his wry smile which to her implied while he was wise to the ways of the world and to women, he was gentleman enough to ignore their stratagems!

They talked for a while and Pilar was surprised at how simple and natural a man Duke seemed. When he left and flew back to Hollywood Pilar found herself wondering if she would ever see Duke again.

At the end of shooting Pilar was sent to Hollywood herself to do some sound track dubbing on her own film. One day, quite by accident, Duke and Pilar bumped into each other in the Green Room restaurant at Warner Brothers where Duke was making a film.

He remembered her instantly. 'Hello there,' he said. 'I remember you! Tingo Maria. Pilar Palette. Will you have dinner with me tonight, Pilar?'

Pilar felt it was a kind of hands-across-the-Panama-Canal good will invitation. And she was, after all, twenty-three years younger than the star. But she was lonely in Hollywood and she liked Duke, so she accepted.

She had dinner with him that night. And she's had dinner with him almost every night since. In fact, she never went back to live permanently in Peru since that first dinner date. It wasn't long before Duke and Pilar knew they were in love and they weren't happy when they were away from each other.

Pilar can't remember Duke ever *formally* proposing to her. One day he took her to see the beautiful rambling old ranch house he owned in Encino just outside Hollywood. It had a three-level garden and a swimming pool down an enormous flight of stone steps. The twenty-room house nestled in its own secluded five acres of hills and wild woodland.

'I bought it in 1950,' Duke said as they stood in the driveway. 'I've hardly lived in it. But if you don't think you'd be happy here, Pilar, I'll sell it and buy a smaller home wherever you like.'

'I could be very happy here with you,' Pilar told him simply. And that was the nearest Duke ever came to making a formal proposal of marriage.

At this time Duke was going through the throes of his divorce from Esperanza Baur and towards the end of that year, before his decree became final, he had to make *The Sea Chase* with Lana Turner in Hawaii. Duke asked Pilar to go along too.

Since she loved him and she knew his secretary would be going too and therefore she'd have both a chaperon and a girl companion, Pilar was thrilled to accept.

She soon learned that life with Duke would be full of surprises. September 3 is her birthday but as no one even said 'Happy Birthday' to her on that day in Hawaii, she felt rather low about it. Her first birthday away from home and not even the man she loved had remembered it!

That afternoon Duke and Pilar went to a cocktail party given by the US Ambassador. It ended about five o'clock and back at the hotel Pilar felt tired and unhappy, so she took off her make-up and said she was going to bed.

But Duke talked her into going for a quiet bite to eat at a restaurant called *The Beachcomber*. Knowing it was a rather dimly lit place, Pilar just put on minimum make-up, not really bothering at all.

Suddenly, as they walked through the door, a large orchestra burst into 'Happy Birthday To You', one whole wall was decorated with flowers saying 'Happy Birthday, Pilar'. Not only were all the cast and crew of their own film there but the entire cast and crew of *Mr Roberts* which was also shooting in Hawaii, and some of Duke's dearest friends like Ward Bond, director Jack Ford and Henry Fonda were also all there to help shower Pilar with congratulations.

'There was champagne, cake and presents,' Pilar remembers, 'and all the time with hardly any make-up on I felt like a ghost. If I hadn't been so delighted that Duke had remembered my birthday after all, I could have murdered him!'

But Duke had far more romantic plans for Pilar in Hawaii. He was hoping against hope that his divorce decree would become final in time for him to marry Pilar in a beautiful Hawaiian setting, preferably in a sunset. But filming gradually came to an end and still there was no news.

On their very last day there – it was 1 November 1954 – Duke and Pilar were having breakfast together when Duke's lawyer rang. 'Your divorce is through,' he said. 'You're a free man!' Duke smiled at Pilar. They both knew that was it. They were married the same night.

Today, when Duke pretends to be mad at Pilar, he sighs and kids her 'You never even gave me one day of freedom. I was a married man at breakfast, single at lunch, and married again by dinner!'

To Pilar it was the most romantic wedding any woman could hope for. Duke's wish to marry her in a sunset came true. It was a gorgeous golden sunset on Hawaii's Kona coast, with the sinking sun making what seemed a path of liquid gold to heaven on the darkening seas as they licked the sand on the silver beaches.

All over the island the natives closed their little shops and came along with their instruments, leis and flowers and played their beautiful aloha music for Duke and Pilar. The island's Judge came over at a few hours' notice from the other end of the island to marry them, and their director John Farrow gave Pilar away.

The same night they flew to Honolulu and then home to the big house at Encino. They reversed the normal honeymoon. Most couples marry at home and then fly to somewhere like Hawaii but beautiful though Hawaii was, their rambling old mansion in Encino was where Pilar wanted to be with Duke.

In those first few months in their secluded home Pilar really began to understand how Duke came to be the man he was. She certainly expected married life with him to be a big challenge. She herself was living away from her home and country for the first time and he had been one of the world's most popular stars long before she'd known of him. But Pilar soon came to realize that whatever else motivated Duke Wayne, the real *raison d'être* of his life was work. It was a compulsion with him. He worked harder than any man she'd ever known and even in his few free moments there were a thousand calls on his time.

Although she had been going out with him for several months, Pilar knew there could be an enormous difference between going out with someone as an unmarried girl – and then settling down with him in the give-and-take relationship of being husband and wife.

She knew of his legendary reputation, of the many stories about the boisterous socializing of Duke with his 'Rolling Stock Company' pals. But any slight trepidation she may have felt was soon dispelled for she found that off screen Duke was the complete family man.

From the start he was solicitous to Pilar's comfort and needs and was overwhelmingly generous – a generosity, however, which did not include throwing wild parties for his friends. Duke's home was his *home*. A base of love and security where his children could grow up normally and well adjusted.

Before their marriage, Pilar had played the lead in two films in Peru. One day Duke asked her 'Do you want to continue as an actress, because if you do I'll help you any way I can?'

He was, nevertheless, relieved when Pilar replied that she'd never really cared for that life. Pilar doesn't believe there can be two stars in a marriage. And she had no desire to be a part time mother.

Pilar still finds Duke's generosity extraordinary.

'He loves nothing more than to go shopping for his family,' she told me. 'And he shops like he works, dynamically. He walks round a store saying "I'd like five of those, three of those..." When he's on location and can't go shopping himself, he takes mail order magazines with him, circles things in them and then tells his secretary to have them sent to us. We sometimes get three packages a day delivered to our door. And we have a small warehouse near us which is full of things Duke has sent which we can't get into the house!'

Duke tells Pilar that he admires her serenity and dignity. 'But it's not always easy to be serene with a man who lives to the full as Duke does,' Pilar laughs. 'He has enormous energy and can get by on four hours sleep a night. Luckily we both can.'

She says Duke isn't the tidiest of men to live with. He seldom puts things back in their places and he often leaves his shirts on chairs and his socks on the floor.

'And he's certainly no handyman. He can't hammer a nail or hang a painting. And he's no gardener either. He can tell you where to hang a picture or what colours to use in a room as he has wonderful taste, but he can't do it himself.'

One of Duke's rare qualities, says Pilar, is that she seldom sees him irritable or depressed. Most days he even wakes up feeling happy.

Early on, Pilar discovered that Duke isn't an overtly religious man. But he does believe in God, a supreme being. When he had his battle with lung cancer in 1964 and had most of his left lung removed, the world's papers were saying how John Wayne had licked the Big C. But Duke said 'I didn't beat it myself – not without good doctors and the Man upstairs.'

Pilar found that in real life, just as in his films, Duke doesn't talk, he *does*. To her his life, the way he lives, is an example.

He never lectures his children. But he told them once: 'Don't judge other people till you know the experiences they've been through. And only then if you can really understand those experiences.'

I asked Duke about this statement once and he looked a bit embarrassed. He hates pomposity or didacticism of any kind.

'Well,' he said, removing his hat and scratching his thinning hair. 'It's hard to pass on experience, you know, kids have to go through it for themselves. But if you've given them something true, later on, when they step out of line, they'll remember the strength of the statement and it'll help them come out of it quicker.'

Duke *is* an old-fashioned father, but in a rare way. He guides rather than instructs. There is an unusually close feeling between Duke and Pilar and all his seven children. It gives the Wayne clan a unique strength which an outsider can feel when they're all together.

After their marriage, both Duke and Pilar wanted to have their own children. Yet Pilar says before the birth of each of their three – Aissa, Ethan and Marisa – Duke's concern for her always bordered on something like panic.

When Aissa was about to be born in March 1956, Pilar woke Duke up in the middle of the night and told him they'd better start for the hospital – St Joseph's in Burbank.

'Now don't get nervous,' he kept saying as they got dressed.

'I wasn't at all nervous,' remembers Pilar. 'But *he* was. Driving me to hospital he kept singing off-key songs, the kind he used to sing with Ward Bond and Jack Ford round campfires in places like Utah. They were meant to calm me, I suppose, but they weren't those kind of songs at all!'

Duke took a left turn instead of a right and when they couldn't find the hospital he almost went to pieces. It annoyed him too because he had lived in the valley most of his life. Luckily Aissa was a few hours late in arriving.

When Duke was first allowed into the hospital room to see

In Howard Hawks' *Rio Bravo*, Duke played Sheriff Chance, as with
Gary Cooper in *High Noon*, defending a town single-handed. But whereas
Gary tried to get help but couldn't, Duke rejected help and ultimately had
to depend on it

Duke directed, produced
and starred in *The Alamo*,
the most ambitious project
of his life. To Duke, the
Alamo, an abandoned
mission where 182 Ameri-
cans sacrificed their lives in
the Texan war for inde-
pendence, was the 'great
American story'

North to Alaska was
Henry Hathaway's
rumbustious comedy
western. Duke played
a gold prospector
who found a wife
instead – here played
by Capucine

his wife and new bouncing 7lb 6oz. daughter, Pilar thought he would say something beautiful and tender, something she would remember for years. But he just sat on the bed, wiped his anxious brow and said 'Move over, I'm pooped!'

It was one of the few times she had seen him tired for Duke Wayne does have a large fund of energy. When most actors have finished scenes, especially on a hot dusty location, they usually retire to their dressing rooms to drink, rest or play chess or cards. But Duke usually stays with the action and the director, not because he wants to run things himself but because after nearly two hundred and fifty films he's still fascinated by the work. And the rougher the location, the more outdoor and camp fire-ish it gets, the more he likes it. Lack of modern conveniences like piped water or electricity doesn't bother him.

Pilar says for her it's been a case of marrying an actor and seeing the world. She has been on his films in England, Japan, Hong Kong, Italy, Africa, France, Hawaii, Mexico and several other countries.

The roughest location for her was when Duke made *Legend Of The Lost* with Sophia Loren and Rosanno Brazzi in north Africa, where they shot scenes at a tiny oasis in the Sahara Desert called Gadames.

Aissa was just a young baby then so Pilar decided to sit that one out at home. But one day a cable arrived from Duke: 'Come over right away.'

'Oh my God, he's sick,' was her first thought. Leaving Aissa in the care of her nanny, it took her nearly three days of hopping on and off planes to get to Gadames and when she arrived Duke was clearly blooming with health.

Pilar looked round at the primitive location, watched Duke throwing water on the mud floor of his hut to stop the dust rising, and said 'Why on earth have you got me all this way?'

Duke just grinned. 'Wait till you see the sunsets!' he said.

But Pilar's compensation came when she had three enjoyable weeks in Rome – while Duke was shooting the interior scenes. She spent much of her time shopping for antiques. But Duke got a ribbing from Rosanno Brazzi for flying his wife out to the desert location. Brazzi had been told it was too rough for women and that *his* wife Lydia could not come!

Pilar never watched Duke's love scenes with his beautiful

co-stars. It's almost a rule with her – not because she's jealous of Duke kissing other women for the cameras but because she feels in the way.

'He'd like me to visit his sets more than I do,' she told me. 'But I feel they're all working hard and it's no place for me. If I sit in a chair it's almost always over a cable that has to be moved somewhere else. And if I'd watched his love scenes with Sophia Loren I'm sure they'd have *both* felt uncomfortable. It's *work*. He *has* to do it, poor fellow!'

Far from being jealous of Duke's screen wives, Pilar tends to make friends with them. In Rome Sophia visited the Waynes' house for dinner.

'Aissa was just a baby at the time and we couldn't get Sophia out of our nursery. She hadn't had her own baby then and I never saw anyone behave with a baby the way she did. She wanted a child so badly, I'm so glad she has her own little boy now.'

And five years later when Pilar went back to Africa to join Duke while he was making the animal adventure epic *Hatari!*, she made a life long friend of Duke's co-star Elsa Martinelli.

'Elsa cooked beautiful Italian dishes for us,' remembers Pilar. 'And after that film she had to do a month's work in Hollywood so she was our house guest for the whole month. When we go to Rome she's the first person we call. No, I'm not jealous of any of his leading ladies.'

During the mid and later fifties Duke made several films which did absolutely nothing to enhance his acting reputation. *Legend Of The Lost* was one of them. Its lack of success didn't help Batjac's fortunes either.

Three more films which came out at this time proved to be pretty mediocre stuff too. One was *Jet Pilot* which producer Howard Hughes had held back from release for eight years and which was funny without intention. In it, Janet Leigh played a Soviet woman jet pilot forced to land on a US airfield and Duke was the American pilot sent to guard her. It contained an impossible scene where tiny Janet knocked out Duke with a fist to the jaw – an item which attracted raucous laughter in movie houses around the world.

Another film which didn't help Wayne's career was *The Barbarian And The Geisha*, directed oddly enough by John

Huston. Badly miscast as Townsend Harris, America's first diplomatic representative to Japan, Wayne, all dressed up in period costume and mouthing meaningless platitudes, looked clearly embarrassed by the whole thing.

The third disappointment in this period was *The Conquerors,* Dick Powell's rather hapless historical epic in which Duke was miscast as Ghengis Khan, complete with divided moustache and made-up slit eyes.

An actor of lesser stature and popularity might well have found his career in ruins after such a trio. But he survived because he made some good films in between them.

Often when Duke was away on location and Pilar had to stay behind with Aissa and, later on, baby Ethan, she found life lonely and uneventful for her in the big isolated old house at Encino. But on one occasion Pilar had a great deal more excitement and action than she wanted.

One night in February 1958 when Duke was away in Kyoto, Japan, making *The Barbarian And The Geisha,* Pilar was suddenly woken up by their pet dachshund Blackie, who jumped on the bed barking.

Pilar tells the story:

'The bedroom and whole house was full of smoke. I leaped out of bed, took baby Aissa from her crib and carried her downstairs. Then I rushed back with the fire extinguisher and opened all the windows to try and clear the smoke – only to find I didn't know how to work the extinguisher.

'I stood there trying to fan the smoke away with my hands so I could read the instructions but I started choking. I realized I might die if I stayed there any longer so I ran back downstairs again.

'It was a very windy night and by the time I'd got down the hall and woken up our two maids, the heat and flames really began. The only thing I managed to grab before I ran out was Duke's old Cavalry hat which he'd worn on nearly every western film for eleven years!'

Pilar just had time to telephone the fire brigade before the smoke forced her outside in her robe, still clutching Duke's hat.

As the firemen from seven tenders trained their hoses on the flames, the chief wasted no time telling Pilar she should

67

never have opened the windows as it causes a draught which fans the fire bigger.

The roof and some of the top floor of the house were gutted but the Waynes turned this to their advantage in the end. As they rebuilt the house, so they modernized it.

And at least Pilar had rescued Duke's beloved hat, though as things turned out later she could have spared herself the effort. Duke lent the hat to Sammy Davis Jr to wear when he made *Sergeants Three* with Frank Sinatra and Dean Martin, and it came back ruined. Apparently every time Sammy had worn it his fellow stars had pulled it down over his ears, saying 'Oh, Duke Wayne huh?'

As Duke sadly and finally dropped his hat into the waste bin, he said 'Hell, maybe I should have made a bronze of it!'

When Duke got back from Japan, Pilar found out he'd been having a spot of fire trouble of his own at the same time. A burning ship they were filming in the harbour had drifted too close to some Japanese fishing boats and had scorched three of them. Duke had led the fight to clear the ship away. Not, however, before some of the Japanese fishermen had come to blows with some of the film crew.

One film that helped restore Duke's tattered acting reputation during the later fifties was Jack Ford's epic western *The Searchers*. In it Duke played Ethan Edwards, a harsh embittered man who returns from a hunt for cattle rustlers to find his brother's family wiped out in a Comanche raid and his two young daughters abducted by the Indians. With his brother's adopted half-breed son in tow (whom Edwards despises) he sets out to find the girls. The search drags on for years, becoming a personal vendetta. In spite of Edwards' rigid unbending nature, Wayne managed to convey the man's tragic loneliness.

He gave a good performance in Ford's next, *The Wings of Eagles,* then topped that with his role as Sheriff T. Chance in Howard Hawks' *Rio Bravo*. Using a similar basic situation – where a sheriff has to defend singlehanded a town against an outlaw band – Duke extracted as much in comedy as Gary Cooper had in drama in his film *High Noon*. Where Cooper pleaded for help from the townsfolk but finally didn't need it, Wayne refused help but ultimately had to depend on it.

All this time, of course, Duke had been planning his own

big picture *The Alamo*. At the end of the fifties his production relationship with the then existing hierarchy at Warner Brothers began to degenerate, so he left them.

'I made ten pictures there which made a great deal of money for them and a great deal for me too,' Duke explained it to me. 'Finally other people there started saying we were getting all the breaks, making too much money. They were going to start changing the terms of the deal so I left and went to United Artists. It was a lesser deal but one which gave me more freedom as a producer.'

Part of that freedom was the backing for Duke to go ahead on his life's most ambitious project, *The Alamo*.

The battle at the Alamo, an abandoned mission where a hundred and eighty-two men sacrificed their lives for liberty against a huge Mexican army during Texas' fight for independence, was more to Duke than an epic tale of heroism and patriotism. Three of the greatest names in the rugged pioneering history of America died there, William Travis, Jim Bowie and Davy Crockett.

'We wanted to re-create a moment in history which will show to this generation of Americans what their country stands for and to put in front of their eyes the bloody truth of what some of their forbears went through to win what they had to have or die – liberty and freedom.

'Freedom and liberty don't come cheaply, not for any people in this world, and if you're put to the torch you have to stand up and fight and even be prepared to die if you have to.'

Duke felt the story had relevance in the western world today, with its freedoms menaced by Communism (as it's practised if not as it's written). *The Alamo* was, he felt, *the* great American story.

Now that he'd at last got the green flag, Duke set to work in earnest. He knew it was going to be a tough, uphill, one-man battle but right then he had little idea of the real troubles looming ahead.

6

THE DISASTER YEARS

In early 1959, as Duke struggled to assemble his stars, fix the right locations, hire the best crew among men he'd worked with all his life for *The Alamo*, he and Pilar were heading for the most trouble-filled years of their lives, though they had no inkling of it at the time.

In the spring Pilar found herself pregnant. Both she and Duke were delighted at the thought of their second child but complications set in and Pilar was taken to hospital. On May 26 – Duke's birthday – she lost the baby.

Doctors told her they could find nothing wrong with her physically and that it was really a psychological problem. This can be fairly common among women who become over-anxious but luckily Pilar suffered no permanent ill effects.

Making *The Alamo* proved to be a complete family enterprise, thus laying the foundation for turning Batjac into the virtual family concern it later became. And Pilar threw her wifely support behind Duke all the way on *The Alamo*. He'd talked about his dream ever since he'd first met her. In fact they'd never have met at all if Duke hadn't gone to Peru scouting locations for it.

Pilar, daughter Aissa, and some of Duke's other children spent three months with him on location in Bracketville, Texas, and worked on the film with him. Aissa made her debut in it, Duke's eldest son Michael was its assistant producer and his second son Patrick co-starred in it with Duke.

Pilar says she went along mostly to ensure Duke didn't drive the rest of the family too hard!

Throughout the three months, Duke was under enormous pressure. He not only starred as Davy Crockett but he produced and directed the whole film from start to finish.

One logistics problem he came up against was that he needed fifteen hundred horses – and he found all the trained Hollywood horses were being rented out on TV series. Duke and his production manager had to comb seven states to get all the animals they needed.

At times Pilar saw how angry Duke could get when things went wrong through someone's carelessness. She saw strong men go pale when he bawled them out for some inefficiency. But as usual his anger was a controlled thing, the opposite of temper. And he was always over it soon and quick to make friends again.

During production Duke needed an extra seven hundred thousand dollars to finish the picture over and above what he'd expected. But a visiting executive from the studio told him 'You won't get it, Duke. They're short of money themselves right now. And you and I know they can't borrow on your movie.'

Duke thought deeply. United Artists had been good to him, had at least let him make the picture and had allowed him to spend half a million dollars before they'd had anything between them on paper. In the end he said 'To hell with it, I'll mortage Batjac.' And he did. Altogether he sank one million, two hundred thousand dollars of his own money into *The Alamo*.

He was exhausted when he directed the final battle scenes in December but he brought the film in for a negative cost of six million five hundred thousand dollars, certainly nothing like the fifteen million dollars the world's Press printed at the time.

Later, Duke told me, he discovered the executive hadn't told him the complete truth. The studio *did* have the money, but clearly felt they were risking enough on the film as it was and didn't want to increase their financial commitment at that point.

When *The Alamo* came out, Jack Ford said 'It's the greatest picture I've ever seen. It will last for ever, run for ever, for all peoples, all families everywhere.' And Ford isn't a man given to generous praise if he doesn't mean it, particularly with friends!

The Alamo was nominated for eleven Oscars but didn't win one. Most critics, however, were not so fulsome in their praise

71

and the picture was less than a smash hit at the box office.

As Duke waited anxiously to see if box office receipts would justify his own faith in his project, top film chief Darryl F. Zanuck gave a Press interview in Paris in which he lashed out at stars who tried to go from acting to producing their own pictures.

'I have great affection for Duke Wayne,' he was reported as saying 'But what right has he got to write, direct and produce a motion picture? What right has Kirk Douglas got, or Widmark or Brando? Look at poor old Duke Wayne – he's never going to see a nickel. He put all his own money into financing *The Alamo....*'

Wayne, on location for another film by now, was stung to a quick cabled reply:

'It is my hope that expatriate American producers shed no crocodile tears over poor old Duke Wayne who thus far in a 30 year star career brought over three hundred million dollars into producers' tills and plans not only to keep on doing this for producers but is doing a little bit of it for himself for a change.....' Pointing out that great producers of the past had come from all walks of the industry, he named over fifty of them and added 'I'm mighty proud to be in that company and I'm proud that my production company made *The Alamo.* Please inform Mr Zanuck that as far as poor old Duke Wayne and his pictures are concerned, which was made in the United States of America, it has made just under two million dollars in three months in thirteen theatres in America and has ten thousand more play dates to go. It's broken records of *Around The World In Eighty Days* in such places as Tokyo, London, Paris and Rome and will end up being one of the highest grossers of all time.'

It was a brave and optimistic defence but on its first release *The Alamo* was clearly *not* one of the highest grossers of all time, and while everyone else involved in the production got paid off, Duke got back precisely nothing.

While many people know *The Alamo* was a financial failure for Duke on its first release, few know about the curious events that followed. Many years later, hoping at least to get back what he'd invested, Duke sold his interest in it back to United Artists. He told me he was so anxious at the time to get his

Duke belts out at his old pal Lee Marvin in *Donovan's Reef*. This shot
illustrates Duke's description of screen fighting 'You have to reach way
back and sock out, but in a real fight you hit short and close. You don't get
time to pull your punches back so far'

A thin, haggard-looking Duke goes to work on *The Sons of Katie Elder*,
the first film he made after his battle with lung cancer. He still did tough
scenes such as being thrown into an icy river

In *The Hellfighters* Duke plays
the part of Texan 'Red' Adair,
a real life fighter of oil field
fires. As special jets were
trained on him to keep him
from being burnt, Duke
gagged 'I'll go in only if Red
tells me it's safe'. Red did

Duke Wayne leads his Green
Berets into action. Duke
produced, directed and starred
in *The Green Berets*. To those
who said he was glorifying an
unpopular war, he replied
'What war was ever popular,
for God's sake?'

Duke, as rascally Marshall Rooster Cogburn in *True Grit* parodies an ageing lawman whose solace is the bottle. At sixty-two he did the dangerous back fall from the horse himself

Duke is down, shaken but unhurt, ready for the next 'take'

money back, he didn't make a very good deal and he should have stuck out for a bigger percentage.

The result was United Artists made a profit of five million dollars on re-run and re-distribution rights. But Duke, apart from getting back his initial capital investment plus that of his friends, got nothing at all for all his hard work as star, producer and director.

The Alamo's failure was a tremendous disappointment to Duke, particularly as it had embodied all his own patriotic ideals. Viewed today, it's hard to understand why its first run was a flop because it was certainly as good as many other epics which had sent box offices jingling. And though not entirely faultless, it remains a considerable achievement for a novice director – as Wayne then was.

The years immediately following *The Alamo* were tough ones for Duke. Several of his business enterprises were showing unhealthy signs – problems which were further aggravated by the fact that the one million two hundred thousand dollars, which consisted mostly of the Batjac mortgage money, was still tied up in *The Alamo* and it didn't look right then as if Duke would ever see a cent of it back.

Emotionally too, the recent deaths of close friends and colleagues sapped him considerably. Actor Grant Withers, one of Duke's 'Rolling Stock Company' buddies, committed suicide, and Duke's long time friend and Press agent, Bev Barnett, also passed away. The worst blow came when his great pal from college days, Ward Bond, dropped dead suddenly in November 1960 from a heart attack while in a shower at Dallas, Texas. Ward's death at only fifty-five really shook Duke – as it also did Jack Ford who'd always reckoned he'd be the first of the group to go.

Duke helped make the funeral arrangements for his old friend and he delivered the eulogy in Jack Ford's private chapel – but Ford himself couldn't be there as he was making a film in Texas.

Duke, who hates funerals anyway, was immensely saddened. 'Ward was a big rough tough guy but he was the kindest man I ever met,' Duke remembers. 'And the solemnity of it all made it worse. I prefer the idea of Irish 'wakes' when all the friends come over to help the family over the hump, have a few drinks or cakes and coffee, and just talk about the good times they had with the deceased. To me the burial ceremony is mediaeval and primeval. I'd prefer to be cremated, anything rather than be buried in that box, or even worse, waking up in it.'

Duke says when he dies his funeral will be out of Ford's little chapel because for him it all began with Ford.

In 1961 he was further saddened by the death from cancer of his beloved colleague Gary Cooper. And it was in that year that Duke found he was having to start all over again financially. After more than two hundred films, his millions had mysteriously slipped away.

Up till the previous year Duke had had a business manager who while he didn't do anything illegal, had involved him in several unfortunate money losing deals. As soon as Duke discovered the real state of his affairs, he broke with the man but that didn't help him recoup the lost fortune he'd spent so long building up.

First there was that huge investment still tied up in *The Alamo*. Then a five hundred thousand dollar shrimp boat business in Panama which was being run by Tony Arias, brother of diplomat Roberto Arias, Margot Fonteyn's husband, struck disaster when Tony was killed in a plane crash on the way to Mexico City.

At one time Duke and Tony Arias were running over seventy per cent of the shrimping business in Panama, but after Tony's death it dwindled to twelve per cent and then finally Duke lost everything.

Tony, who died while on his way to perform a personal favour for Duke, was a great friend of the Waynes and he was also Aissa's godfather. So his death was a doubly tragic blow.

Another enterprise which folded around this time was a whisky importing firm in which Duke was partner with actor Bruce Cabot and Prince Bernhard of The Netherlands. Several of his other businesses, which included apartment houses, taxi franchises and oil wells, were also in the red.

And all the while Duke was maintaining a staff on full salary at his offices just off Hollywood's Sunset Strip – even though Batjac was inactive for several years after *The Alamo*.

One of Duke's colleagues, the late scriptwriter James Edward Grant, who scripted many of Wayne's best films, once said Duke's trouble was partly that he was a sucker for a hard luck story.

'He has spent over a million bucks on his friends, or even on guys who claim they went to school with him,' said Grant. 'One guy came along and talked Duke into putting up thousands to raise a sunken vessel. It was supposed to be loaded with copper ingots. Duke never saw his money again. Once when a cop stopped him for speeding, he talked him into investing in a sugar sack factory in South America. One alcoholic actor guy cost Duke over seventy thousand dollars in sanatorium treatment over several years. It makes me want to shoot him!'

Pilar also told me 'I know Duke has probably spent a million dollars on friends, or on the projects of friends, and has in the past trusted men who have given him bad advice. But he would never chase a friend for the return of money lost in this way, or sue anyone.'

Duke's answer to his problems in the early sixties was characteristic – work. Brooding over personal tragedy or material loss is not in his make-up. He took charge of his own business affairs from then on and just went into picture after picture, working at a pace which could have prostrated a much younger man.

'It *was* a hard time back then,' Duke remembers. 'Before it all, on paper, I was supposed to be worth four or five million (dollars) and suddenly I found I didn't have a goddam thing. If I'd sold everything then I'd have just about broken even. That means broke, but it didn't change my manner of living.'

Taking no gambles when it came to recouping his fortunes, he made five western style pictures one after the other. *The Horse Soldiers* for Jack Ford, a Civil War spectacular in which he and William Holden were paid seven hundred and fifty thousand dollars each, the highest fees ever paid to actors up to that time. Again Duke played an ageing western hero with deceptive ease.

He made the entertaining and unpretentious *The Comman-cheros* – playing a Texas ranger who joins up with a gambler to wipe out a secret bunch of renegades – went on a long tough location in Henry Hathaway's *North To Alaska*, then gave a significant performance as a tough old gun fighting rancher in Jack Ford's *The Man Who Shot Liberty Valance*.

He was working so hard now, dashing out at dawn and

returning exhausted at night, that Pilar who had been his wife and living continuously in America for eight years, decided to visit her homeland.

'For a long time I had felt a little homesick and I kept saying to Duke "I can't wait to visit home again. The weather is better, my friends are wonderful, we have the best music in Peru, the best restaurants..." and so on. So finally, when Duke was working on *North To Alaska*, which I remember as the *muddiest* film he ever made because his big boots traipsed mud all over the house, and he was about to leave on a really rough location, he said "All right, go back and stay with your family awhile." '

Pilar flew back to Lima, eager to see her mother at home and her old friends again, but after a few days she felt like a complete stranger there. She was suddenly a complete outsider. All her friends were now married and had their own lives to lead. She only stayed four days then she flew right back to California, knowing it was now her home and where she wanted to live for the rest of her life.

Shortly after this Pilar took out American citizenship papers. She says though that Duke never put any pressure on her to change her nationality, one way or the other, because he knew it was a very important decision and had to be hers alone.

Their happiest moment at this time was when Pilar found she was going to have another baby. For six years after Aissa she'd been trying to have another child, so after her miscarriage in 1959 she wasn't taking any chances. She had long talks with her doctor, Dr Delmar Mitchelson, and she obeyed his instructions to the letter.

Duke was hoping for a son this time and he also wanted to be at home with Pilar when the baby was born. Making a cameo appearance in Zanuck's *The Longest Day* in France at the time, he swore he'd hold up the picture for a couple of days if he had to in order to be with her in time!

As it happened, he was back in Encino over a week before the birth.

But they were having a hard problem choosing a name. If Pilar had a boy she wanted to call him Michael — because Michael had been her father's name, was her brother's name and also it was one of Duke's real names — Marion Michael

Morrison. But Duke didn't like it as he already had a son called Michael. So Michael as a name was out.

One evening Duke and Pilar were sitting at home watching TV when on came *The Searchers*, one of Pilar's favourite westerns. As they watched Duke playing the part of the lone Ethan Edwards, Pilar said 'That's it! If we have a boy, let's call him Ethan.'

They both laughed and Duke said 'Wonderful. I love it.'

So that's how, when Pilar did indeed give birth to a baby boy on 23 February 1962, he was given the unusual name of Ethan.

By now Duke wasn't sparing himself at all, was almost running from film to film as if he felt his time as an actor was running out. He divided his time between war films, westerns and adventure films.

When he made *Hatari!* the first of the 'African westerns', Duke had some dangerous work to do so he left on his own, a month before Pilar joined him. During one location scene a wild rhino charged the Land Rover he was in and dented the metal work.

'I'm glad I wasn't there to see that,' says Pilar, 'even though I know he has adequate protection in such scenes. But it was a wonderful location as it was in a really primeval part of east Africa. I liked it too because he wasn't killing the animals, only roping them. It isn't easy to rope a wild rhino but in that scene in the film Duke didn't have any stunt men, he did that roping himself.'

Duke also shot a charging elephant while on that picture. One shot between the eyes and it dropped in its tracks. This dastardly deed was kept out of the papers, however.

'They got it all on film because the camera was right behind me,' Duke says. 'A great sequence but we couldn't use a foot of it in the final film. John Wayne shot a poor elephant? I guess they felt it would destroy my heroic image or something.'

In Duke's picture gallery at home is a photo of Pilar and Aissa standing in front of the huge dead fallen elephant, their noses wrinkled. Its head alone is taller than they are.

'They needed a scene of a dead elephant that was supposed to have been shot by a white hunter,' Duke recalls. 'So they loaded my elephant on a flat-bed trailer and towed it over two hundred miles to the main location site. They shot the damn thing full of formaldehyde to stop it rotting, but that picture was taken after five days. The stench was unbelievable.'

Duke appeared briefly as General Sherman in the first big Cinerama production *How The West Was Won,* in an episode directed by Jack Ford. Then Ford hired him for *Donovan's Reef,* which was virtually a re-make of *The Quiet Man* in a South Seas setting. In it Duke and Lee Marvin played two ex-US Navy pals who retire to a south Pacific island. When a young Boston socialite, Elizabeth Allen, comes into their lives, Donovan first knocks the pride and snobbery out of her, then falls in love with her.

Donovan's Reef was lightweight Ford and it seems a pity this may be the last film Ford and Wayne make together, in view of all the great pictures on which they've collaborated in the past. But Ford is now past his mid seventies and since his illness when making *The Young Cassidy* in 1965, he has been mostly inactive.

In the early and mid sixties Duke's acting work was rather disappointing, partly because at first he was restricting his screen appearances to shorter cameo roles while he rejuvenated his production company, Batjac, a major task in itself. Partly also because of his bout with lung cancer in 1964 when he nearly lost his life, but more of that later.

Duke thought twice about playing the tough circus boss Matt Masters in *The Magnificent Showman* (called *Circus World* in America) but his old colleague, the veteran director Henry Hathaway, wanted Duke and no one else. And 'Hank' Hathaway is a hard man to refuse.

On that picture Duke narrowly missed severe injury. He was filming in Madrid in a huge burning tent and in the scene he was knocking down circus seats with an axe, with the camera behind him and the raging fire in front of him. Hathaway shouted 'Fire. More fire!' A little man playing a clown suddenly ran away and Hathaway yelled at him for spoiling the scene. The clown hollered back that it was so hot he couldn't stand it any more. Duke, who wasn't going to let Hathaway have that on *him,* gritted his teeth and moved in closer, still banging away at the seats with his axe.

Suddenly he realized the scene had been running an awfully

long time. He felt heat on the back of his neck although he was wearing a large hat. He looked up and saw the tent was on fire for about fifty feet behind him and great chunks of burning canvas were hitting the ground. If one of them had hit him it would have been curtains. So he ran forward, away from the flames, and when he got out he saw the camera had been abandoned.

'No one yelled or even threw a rock to warn me or anything,' he snorted later. 'At least, I didn't hear anything. Their first reaction when the burning canvas started to fall was to take off fast!'

But Wayne thrives on danger and plenty of action. 'Keeps the adrenalin flowing,' he said once. And on *McLintock!*, the next film Batjac produced, he made sure fast action was the order of the day.

There was a spectacular mud fight in the film in which Duke and Maureen O'Hara started out hurling mud at each other then wound up, together with half the cast, in one vast mud bath.

The scene took three days to shoot, a cold north wind was blowing all the time and everyone had to stand around draped in blankets for warmth as for continuity reasons they couldn't scrape the mud off between shots. They all caught colds but the fight looked great on the screen.

McLintock! was a highly successful picture, one of Duke's personal favourites, and its making showed how Batjac had now become a closely knit family concern.

Duke and his eldest son Michael co-produced the film. Duke and second son Patrick were the co-stars. Daughter Aissa had a featured role, and the director was Andy McLaglen, the son of the late Victor McLaglen, Duke's lifelong pal. Andy has now been making films with Duke since he was sixteen.

In one shot Duke was supposed to perform a dangerous leap from a twenty foot high roof on to a passing hay wagon. Producer Michael thought a stunt man ought to do it. Duke, who thought he heard Mike use the words 'the old man', said 'to hell with a stunt man. *I'll* do it!'

He sailed off the roof but hit the base of his spine on the hard wooden edge of the wagon. Suffering agonies he got down with a big smile because he wasn't going to let on to his son that he'd been hurt!

Pilar was angry when she heard about the incident. After all, Duke was now fifty-six and at an age where most big money actors, tired of the grind, were managing motels, oil wells, apartment houses and other enterprises bought for them by far-sighted managers.

'I'd rather not know about these things,' she told me once. 'I could never have talked him out of it anyway. I know how he is, once he makes up his mind to do something he does it regardless.'

In early 1964 the Waynes felt it was time they went on a holiday together and enjoyed themselves. So with daughter Aissa and baby Ethan, then just two, they took off on a fishing holiday well away from the cares and pressures of film work. Duke's pastimes mostly consisted of riding, hunting in the high Sierra mountains, or fishing for the big marlin off the coast of Mexico or the Baja, California, in his huge yacht, *The Wild Goose*.

To call Duke's boat a yacht is a gross understatement. It is in fact a converted minesweeper, one hundred and thirty-six feet long, with luxury staterooms and a crew of half a dozen. For years Duke had owned a seventy-three foot motor sailer called *The Nor'wester* but it gave him, he said, 'no pride of possession', so shortly after Ethan was born he had sold it and bought *The Wild Goose*.

When he's not using it for holidays or fishing trips, Duke leases it out. It has been chartered for ventures like oil exploration in Alaskan waters and with its special helicopter flight deck it is basically a work boat rather than a recreational toy.

But the Waynes hadn't been on holiday for more than a few days when tragedy struck. Anchored off the coast of the Baja peninsula one day, they let their crew have the day and night off to go ashore for a local fiesta. On their way back to the yacht later, three of the crewmen were drowned when their 14 foot boat capsized. One man fell overboard trying to change places and in the ensuing confusion of getting him back on board the whole boat overturned.

Three of the men who were good swimmers decided to strike out for the shore but in the treacherous currents they didn't make it. The only survivor was a young man who couldn't swim and who clung to the upturned boat until he was found. He was Efren Montes, the son of the Waynes' cook and man-servant Fausto Montes, who has been in Pilar's service for twenty-two years, since before she married Duke.

Upset by the tragic accident – the boys were also personal friends and were great favourites with their children – Duke and Pilar cut their holiday short and returned home.

Two months later the Waynes received another shock when Duke's son Michael and his younger brother, Bob Morrison, were involved in a car accident in Burbank. Both went to hospital with severe injuries. Mike had a broken leg, a fractured pelvis and broken ribs and when blood clotting set in he was on the acute danger list for a time. He was in hospital for most of that year.

With Mike slowly recovering, Duke plunged himself back into strenuous activity, working to set up no fewer than five new movies. With his plans well afoot, he went off to Honolulu to star in a film about Pearl Harbour, Otto Preminger's *In Harm's Way*.

It was a tough location, with Duke involved in most of the strenuous battle scenes. But when he got back, Duke and Pilar might well have been excused for believing this latest troubled period was at an end.

But towards the end of that year, as if fate were inexorably settling some personal grudge against him, the star who had conquered countless dramatic crises in his films, found himself in a real life script the ending of which, ninety-five times out of a hundred, was death.

7

SHOWDOWN WITH CANCER

For years, ever since his college football days had ended when a surfing wave had torn his shoulder, Duke had been a heavy smoker, often getting through five packets a day.

So when in September 1964 he developed a persistent cough he put it down to his smoking. He reckoned a winter fishing trip to the clear sea air off Mexico would probably do the trick.

But when his cough became worse, Pilar was worried. She told Duke he ought to see his doctor but at first he just laughed and did nothing.

Every year, for film insurance purposes, Duke used to go to the Scripps Clinic in La Jolla for a physical check-up. But he had now been a year and a half without one and Pilar finally convinced him it would be a good idea to go along before his holiday.

He went – and they found a patch on his lung. Further tests proved it was a tumour, and malignant.

As he sat on the bed and put his shirt back on and the doctors talked to him gravely, Duke felt his first stab of fear. The kind of fear a man feels when he's seldom been sick a day in his life. He stood up, trying hard to be John Wayne and said gruffly 'You trying to tell me I've got cancer? Don't lie to me. Let me have the truth. I don't want to be under any illusions.'

So they told him. He had cancer of the left lung. But they felt that with an operation they had a good chance of curing it. What they didn't tell him was that in a case as far advanced as his that chance was no better than one in twenty.

It was a terrible shock and he drove home in a numbed state. He felt, he said, 'as if someone had hit me across the gut with a baseball bat'. That evening he stood on his patio looking out at the valley and up at the mountains he'd lived in most of his life. Everything suddenly seemed precious to him – little things like the breeze wafting through the tops of his trees, a bird flying over a distant peak, the sound of Pilar's voice talking to young Ethan. He was scared, really scared, but deep down he felt an enormous inner resistance to the thought of dying.

I once asked Duke if he could describe how he felt that night and this is what he said:

'I don't know why but I kept thinking more about my wife and kids and did I have things in order for them? And how was I going to break the news to Pilar? So many things come into your mind you don't have time to think about death itself too much. I knew I had a good surgeon. My own lawyer had had it too and pulled through okay with this same surgeon.

'I felt confident somehow but I knew it was going to be an awful rough go. But you're kind of in a state of shock. When a car is bearing down on you, that's one thing. It's self preservation and you leap aside. But a thing like cancer kind of numbs you. You've heard about this terrible thing so long and suddenly a doctor says it, "You've got cancer."'

Duke entered the Good Samaritan Hospital in Los Angeles on September 16 to have the operation.

Pilar, naturally, was terribly worried but she never once broke down in front of Duke. She realized the last thing he needed at that time was a tearful, overwrought wife. She did her best, if not to be cheerful, at least optimistic and to give him all the support, love and encouragement she could.

She went to her church with their children and prayed for his recovery. She had faith too that a man with Duke's will and desire to live would pull through safely.

Duke's studio advisers felt the very word *cancer* was too closely associated with death. Not only did they feel it was bad for Duke's heroic 'image' as a man who was larger than life but if he came through the ordeal, there was no need for anyone to know he'd ever had cancer, they reasoned. Accordingly, they released a story to the Press that Duke had gone into hospital for an old ankle injury, that lung congestion had developed and the surgeons had also removed an abscess from his lung. At the time Duke was under sedation and he was in no condition to deny or even care about what was being published in the world's newspapers about him.

One thought that did plague Duke was that even if he did get through alive, he might be left a helpless invalid, with his loved ones feeling pity and sympathy for him. That he could not have endured.

He had the operation and the doctors were satisfied with it but shortly afterwards oedema complications set in and parts of Duke's body began to swell up.

Pilar, who spent every moment she could at Duke's bedside, recalls 'It was awful because his face swelled up so much you couldn't see his eyes. One eyelid swelled up so much it covered almost half his face. Then that would subside and his neck would swell up. I was terribly worried then and the doctors decided another operation was necessary.'

Fortunately the second operation was a complete success and after a few weeks Duke was on the mend. As soon as he started feeling well enough to watch TV, he wanted to go home. He didn't like the hospital routine, things like being woken up at five in the morning to be handed a glass of iced water, and he hated being isolated away from his family. After a few weeks the doctors released him into Pilar's care and he went home.

It wasn't until that day, when they got back to the big house together and closed the door, that Pilar finally broke down in front of her husband. But they were tears mainly of relief. Duke didn't have a professional nurse at home during his four months recuperation. Pilar nursed him herself because that was the way he wanted it. And he kept his sense of humour. 'This is the longest rest I've had in thirty years,' he quipped to one visitor.

'He was far from being a difficult patient,' Pilar observes. 'I expected it to be far worse. For the first few weeks he was in considerable pain but I didn't hear him complain once.'

Those first few weeks at home in bed were black days for Duke because he hates being confined in any way. His doctors had told him to remain totally inactive for at least six months, until the huge scar on his chest and back had completely healed.

But Pilar found keeping a man like Duke down wasn't easy. In fact it was impossible. He soon got tired of being around the house. Being an invalid isn't him at all. He is a man who needs to spend much of his time in the great outdoors just to keep his spirits toned up. Inside two months Duke was up on his feet and once he could walk again and he and Pilar could get down to their yacht in Newport Beach, he improved quickly.

One of the first things Duke did when he got back on his feet in December was to put the record straight. He hates lies of any kind and he called a Press conference at his home and told the reporters straight out that he *had* had cancer but now he was cured.

'My advisers all told me the public doesn't want its movie heroes associated with serious illnesses like cancer, it destroys their image,' he told them. 'Well, I don't care much about "images" and anyway, I would have thought there was a lot better "image" in the fact that John Wayne had cancer and licked it.' He thought a moment than added 'But I didn't beat it on my own, not without good doctors and the Man upstairs.'

He answered every question the reporters put to him because he believed his own recovery might help to inspire and encourage other people who developed cancer.

'I was saved by early detection,' he said. 'I don't care if I never sell another ticket at the box office but I'm telling the truth so some poor soul somewhere will get a check-up with his doctor and be as lucky as I was. And more men ought to listen to their wives when they beg them to see their doctors. It was Pilar who talked me into getting that routine physical examination. She probably saved my life.'

Today Duke is completely cured. He goes for tests every six months and he is completely clear. And although he'd smoked heavily for forty years he religiously obeyed his doctors' instructions to give up smoking. 'Nothing's easier when you've had the Big C,' he said. Today he just chews tobacco – or gum.

It took him a while after the operation to adjust to his reduced breathing capacity. He had to learn to breathe differently.

Once the truth got around that he had been operated on for cancer there were naturally many people who felt Duke couldn't possibly be really fit. After similar operations many people had been left little better then invalids, the arms on the side where their lungs had been removed hanging semi-paralysed for years. So the rumours began: 'Well, of course they'd *say* he was fit. But an operation as serious as that? On a man Duke's age? ... '

But any doubts as to Duke Wayne's fitness at this time were soon dispelled on the night of 2 January 1965, when a twenty-two-year-old would-be burglar, Dennis Lee Parker, pulled up outside the Wayne home in a taxi, told the driver to wait and crept across the lawn and broke into the house. The suspicious cabby drove away quickly and called the police.

Nine-year-old Aissa heard the intruder first and ran to wake her father. Duke leaped out of bed, pulled on his pants and chased the burglar through the house and across the gardens – straight into the arms of the waiting police who had just arrived at the gate.

The man tried to tell the police that *he* was John Wayne, a story somewhat hard to subtantiate when the real life Duke Wayne was breathing down his neck.

But at least there was one man around that night who could testify that Duke was still a man of action!

To cap it all, when the cabby insisted on being paid, the burglar was broke. So Duke forked out the twenty dollars fare – which included a generous tip for the cabby calling the police.

Two days after that incident, Wayne flew to a rugged mountain location near Durango, Mexico, for what he called 'A real ridin', jumpin' and fightin' picture – *The Sons of Katie Elder*'. It was the toughest picture he'd been offered and he chose to make it for two reasons. First, he was anxious to get back to work and take his mind off what he called 'The Wound' – a twenty-inch scar across his chest and back – and secondly, he wanted to counteract the rumours where people were saying 'poor old Duke – he's finished.'

To reporters who asked him if he was really fit, he drawled, very much in character, 'I'd better be. I didn't get famous for making drawing room comedies!'

None of Duke's pictures are easy to make but *Katie Elder* had special problems. Not only did he have more action scenes himself than in most films, but they were shooting at a height of eight thousand feet. *Any* exercise at that height would have been a strain but for Duke, having to get used to using less than one and a quarter lungs, it was a double strain.

To be on the safe side and on the advice of his doctors, he

took an oxygen inhalator with him for a quick lift when he needed it, but in fact he rarely used it.

'I thought he went back to work much too soon and I was worried for him,' Pilar remembers. 'A week later I flew out to join him in Durango. It was the first time I'd ever left the children to go on location but I went because I knew he wasn't up to peak fitness.'

In one scene Duke had to stage a fight under a bridge in which he got thrown into the icy Rio Chico river. He could have used a stunt man but he didn't because it would then have had to be done in long shot and it would have spoilt the action, which is far more exciting and real in close-up.

The other men in the scene were much smaller and wore rubber suits under their clothes. But Duke couldn't, not only because they don't make skin suits in his size but because he's so big anyway that a rubber suit under his clothes would have made him look completely out of proportion on the screen. It was winter time and they shot that scene for five days and most of the time they were all wet and cold.

After one exchange of blows which ended in him getting thrown into the river, Duke suffered a temporary black-out. But a few quick draughts from the inhalator and he came out of it all right, grinning as usual. At least he didn't end up with a cold like most of the others.

The Press were curious, of course, and reporters came to the location from all over the world. Once as they were gazing at him, he slung a couple of cold-preventing ascorbic acid pills into his mouth, washed them down with a swig from a half gallon jar of mexcal – which is 120 proof and called La Gasolina by the locals – shut his eyes, shook his head and bellowed 'Goddam, I'm the stuff men are made of!'

The twinkle in his eye showed he wasn't only sending them up, he was sending himself up. And Ralph Volkie, Duke's personal trainer for sixteen years, growled in front of the newspapermen 'Duke's got his punch back, I can tell you. The hardest right hand punch I've ever seen.'

He had his appetite back too. Told by his doctors to keep to a twelve hundred calorie diet, he sent his plate back for a second helping once with the words 'Hell, I'm not going round like a sick Beagle when everyone else is eating like crazy.'

Duke found the most painful thing was getting on a horse. Using his left arm and leg exerted pressure on the whole area of his operation and it hurt. As he said, 'I have to mount like a *cheechako* (tenderfoot). It's tough but what the hell. Let's break the adhesions and get back into stride!'

It was enough for most people that old Duke was back in the saddle. One thing that astonished him was the number of letters of sympathy he received from all over the world – they had to stop counting at fifty thousand.

Tragedy that doesn't actually cripple a man can often be beneficial. It makes him kinder, more sensitive and sympathetic to the misfortunes of others.

And Duke admits that after it all he began to discover depths of goodness and understanding in his many acquaintances that he'd never before suspected.

His bout with cancer also proved to him that he was himself by no means invulnerable. And when he got home to Pilar and the children after the film, he really began to take stock of his life in a way he'd never done before.

8

RENASCENCE

One evening Duke looked across the dinner table at his wife and said 'You know something, Pilar? We should completely reorganize our lives. Let's make a fresh start.'

Pilar, who had also been feeling a complete change would do them both good, agreed.

First they put their home up for sale. They had been living in the rambling old house at Encino throughout the whole ten years of their marriage. While it housed many happy memories it had been their home during unhappy experiences too.

Duke told me one of the reasons behind his desire to sell the house: 'I was taking a good hard look at my life and I realized if anything happened to me, leaving that big sprawling place to Pilar wasn't the best thing I could do for her. It was either worth a hell of a lot to someone who wanted it for seclusion, or it was a big white elephant unless you were making a lot of money, which Pilar wouldn't be if I went.'

But putting the house up for sale was only the start.

They decided to build a brand new home for themselves down at Newport Beach where Duke had been spending holidays since about the age of twelve and where they kept their yacht. Duke made plans to move his offices from just off the Sunset Strip to the Paramount lot, to completely remodernize *The Wild Goose,* and he started negotiating new film contracts for the next five years, the first of which was with Paramount. (A wise decision as it was with them that Duke made *True Grit* which won him the 1970 Oscar).

'We thought at first it would take a long time to sell the Encino mansion,' said Pilar. 'It had more than twenty rooms, a three-level garden and five acres of its own land. There were about fifty-five steep steps down to the pool and fifty-five steeper steps back up! You really had to plan things if you went for a swim. It was hard to take care of too and needed a full time gardener just to keep the area round the house respectable. It was a big responsibility.'

Another point was that the Waynes were seldom home together. Either Duke would be away on a rough location alone or Pilar would take the young children, if the location wasn't *too* rough, and join him there. But now Aissa was going to school and Ethan was approaching school age, Pilar would have to stay at home more. Certainly Duke didn't want his children to miss school. Nor, presumably, did the school authorities. So on all counts the Waynes would be far better off living down at Newport, in a smaller place near a good school, where they had plenty of good friends.

Luckily at the time Walt Disney's daughter was looking for an estate like the Wayne's and she bought it. But when Duke first broke this news to Pilar she had last-minute qualms.

'I was still very fond of the place in spite of everything,' she recalls. 'And I tried to get in touch with the Disney people and say I wasn't sure about it yet, but by then it was too late!'

When the time came for the Waynes to move out, Duke did a thoughtful thing. Knowing his wife was still half in love with the house, he said to her one morning 'Why don't we drive down to Newport for the day?' Unsuspecting, Pilar said 'Fine.' They drove down there and Duke had rented a bungalow in the grounds of a hotel near the piece of land on which their new home was being built. After a few hours there and dusk not far away, Pilar said 'When are we going back to Encino?'

'We're *not* going back,' said Duke with a grin. 'I told the movers to go in this morning! But don't worry about a thing. Every room is being packed separately so you'll know where everything is when it arrives here.'

Pilar was thankful for her husband's considerate action. 'I'm glad he did it that way, painlessly, because if I'd gone back to Encino then, the sight of the place again would have brought back so many good memories I would probably have changed my mind and never have left. We'd probably still be there. I had to thank him for the way he did that. He is very far-sighted that way and often tries to save me from any problems or upsets.'

Today, Pilar says, she is glad they made the move because she enjoys her life at the beach far more. At Newport all the shops are only five minutes away. She has made many new friends of her own and has taken up tennis seriously. The children have become fine swimmers and water skiers and they like their schools too. 'Living down here is really like one long weekend,' she says.

As soon as Walt Disney's daughter bought their house she wanted to move into it straightaway. As it was summer time the Waynes decided to try living on *The Wild Goose* for a while. But after a month Pilar decided life on the boat was too risky because Ethan was only three then and she couldn't take the strain of him running up and down the big boat's gangways and possibly falling into the water. So they moved back into the hotel bungalow while their new house was being completed.

Duke set to work ripping out the ceilings in the boat and putting in new ones which were six feet eight inches high. At six feet four, he was tired of having to stoop below decks. He also restructured the master stateroom with its seven by seven foot bed, and supervised the new decorations.

This was now the busiest and most hectic period of the Waynes' lives. Everything was being done at once. Their house was being built right on the beach with magnificent views over Newport Harbour. The boat was being modernized. Duke was moving his offices and working hard on his new film deals and contracts for several years ahead. They were living in bohemian style in a rented bungalow and right in the middle of it all, Pilar discovered she was going to have another baby.

Duke, of course, was delighted. Setting about his new projects with the energy of a young man who'd just got his first big break, he regarded the new baby as a final blessing. But little Marisa was a great surprise for the Waynes as another child hadn't been in their plans or even thoughts. Luckily they were able to move into the new house a few months before Marisa was born. But only the main rooms had been completed and they were still rearranging all their furniture around as the builders finished the last stages.

Duke, as was usual when Pilar became pregnant, began to worry again. This time it was about the long sixty mile drive back into town. Although he could cover it in an hour up the freeway, he felt it was too far to drive if any emergency occurred. Pilar wanted to have Marisa at the West Valley Hospital in Encino where she knew some of the staff and she could have Dr Delmar Mitchelson who had looked after her through Aissa's and Ethan's births. Duke felt it would be more sensible to get the doctor down to Newport so Pilar could have the baby at home.

But Pilar's mind was made up – she wanted to have her baby in hospital again. Finally Duke told her 'Well, I'm not going to drive you there. You'll just have to get someone else. I won't do it.' No doubt he was also probably remembering the time he drove Pilar to hospital to have Aissa and lost his way!

Just before Marisa was due and Duke was working on a new film, Pilar drove up to see her doctor. Dr Mitchelson examined her and said 'You'd better check into hospital right away because any time now you'll be in labour. It could be this evening but you're very close.'

Pilar, however, felt fine and she said 'No, I want to go and pack a few things first and make sure everything is organized at the house.'

When she got back Duke had just arrived home from work and she told him what her doctor had said. Duke winced. Pilar gave her maid some last minute instructions then went upstairs to pack. She took her time over it as she was feeling really good but she says that Duke just went all to pieces again.

'He waited impatiently at the wheel of the car for almost an hour before I was ready to go. He was just terrified that baby would arrive on the freeway going to the hospital. Then, when he learned he would have to take the other children up with us and book into a hotel with them because we didn't know exactly when baby was arriving, that really made his day! I think he drove us there in about two minutes flat! I felt just great, though, and I knew Marisa wouldn't arrive so soon, but Duke was almost having fits!'

Marisa arrived safely enough, weighing six pounds and fourteen ounces, and Pilar says she looked exactly like Duke.

Despite such moments of trauma before each birth, Duke adores his children. Pilar says he would be happy if she had a dozen more! But she thinks three is enough. They keep her busy and she doubts if she could handle any more.

In the Wayne home most of the disciplining of the children is left to Pilar. Duke's attitude is that he's away filming so much of the time that when he gets home he's entitled to spoil them! Once, when Pilar felt Aissa had misbehaved, she punished her by telling her she couldn't see the film *Romeo and Juliet* which they were showing to some friends and their daughter in their projection room.

But Duke said 'You can't do that. Let her see it, otherwise the other little girl will feel out of place.' Naturally, Aissa saw the film.

Pilar says that for a big powerful man Duke is extraordinarily gentle at home. He is sentimental too – Pilar has never known him forget an anniversary or a birthday. He delights in surprising his family and comes home laden with presents of all kinds. Both Aissa and Ethan have their own horses – birthday presents from Duke. And when she is old enough Marisa will get one too.

When Duke was making *The Undefeated* with Rock Hudson Pilar took some of their neighbourhood friends down to visit him on his earlier scenes in Durango, Mexico. Weeks later Duke arrived home with a box of gold serviette rings he'd had made, not only for his family but for the neighbours too and some tennis friends of Pilar's. Every ring was engraved inside with each person's name. And he'd gone to the trouble of finding out each one of their children's names too. Pilar says this kind of thing is typical of him.

One could say such actions must come easily to a star who earns the kind of money Wayne does. The answer to that is there are a lot of other stars who earn fortunes who aren't so thoughtful.

There is no doubt Duke's gentleness at home and his talent for being considerate are qualities that have helped endear all his children to him. In his staunch, unchangeable character, they've had a father they can easily respect. Mike, Toni, Patrick and Melinda, his four children by his first marriage, are all married with children of their own, having made Duke a granddad no fewer than sixteen times.

Their attitude to Duke was once well summed up by Toni when she said 'He's never been just a pal to us. He's our father and to him we all listen.' The men of the family frankly admire him as a man. Several years ago Michael told the story of when Duke and he sailed the family yacht across the Atlantic from Bermuda to Lisbon.

'My father is absolutely fearless. When we were off the coast of Spain we hit one of the most violent Atlantic storms in years. Some of the crew, all Navy veterans, were down on their bunks praying. My father was up on deck, loving every minute of it.' The truth is that Duke is as proud of them as they are of him.

The Waynes don't see as much of their married children as they would like since they moved out of town and went to live at Newport Beach. But the families visit each other as often as they can. There are so many of them, with so many 'in-laws', that they don't see each other at all over Christmas. That's a holiday every family in the Wayne clan spends with its own 'in-laws'. But shortly after Christmas they all go down to Newport for the once yearly big family gathering with Duke beaming among them all, the beloved patriarch.

He and Pilar have a hard job remembering all their grandchildren's names, never mind knowing which child is which. This is the countdown on the Wayne family:

Michael, who is a producer with Duke's film company, Batjac, is married to Gretchen and they have five children – Alicia, Teresa, Maria, Josephine and Christopher Michael. Toni is married to Donald Le Cava, who as President of Markab Management helps Duke with his business affairs, and they have seven children – Anita, Mark, Bridget, Christopher, Peter, Kevin and (at time of writing) a new baby. Patrick, who majored in biology and is also an actor, is married to Peggy Hunt and they have two children – Michael Ian and Melanie. And Melinda is married to Bob Munoz, a lawyer, and they also have two – Mathew and Laura.

'We don't bother with our grandchildren's birthdays any more,' says Pilar. 'How could we? There are just too many to remember. One Christmas we were packing up presents for all the children and we only did five for Toni's family. Suddenly we realized they had six!'

But that's still not the whole clan. Duke's mother, now married to a popular man called Sid Preem, lives at Long Beach which is near the Waynes and they frequently visit her. She is a tiny woman and though just in her eighties she is still vivacious and full of energy. And Pilar's mother who lives in Lima and is widowed (Pilar's father died of a heart attack at fifty) visits and stays with the Waynes every year.

It's quite a home to visit, too. For a star of Wayne's earning capacity it isn't over large though, as it only has four bedrooms, but it is beautifully designed and the two main living rooms are vast. One looks out over the entire Newport harbour and when the yachts have their red and white spinnakers out and sail slowly past in the sun, it's a magnificent sight. The Waynes have their own jetty beside their lawn which stretches down to the sea and on which Duke likes to play with his children.

The main rooms have quiet gold carpets which set off superbly the unusual antiques the Waynes have gathered in their trips around the world. Pilar is fond of oriental art, particularly of the Ming and T'ai $_3$ dynasties. There are several ancient Chinese tapestries on the walls, and ornaments from Thailand, Japan and China, plus fragile porcelain and stone horses from 900 BC and similar rare pieces.

Pilar is proud of a red lacquer Chinese secretaire which she has converted into a small bar in the front room. They have another black Chinese cabinet which she bought in London – where she believes the world's best antiques can be found – which sets off one wall beautifully. They wanted to make their dining room functional yet not detract from the rest of the house, so they fitted movable Japanese screen doors to it. There are rare pre-Columbian *objets d'art* in there too from Peru and Mexico.

They have made their house elegant and luxurious but also restful and comfortable. Ferns, rubber trees and oriental pot plants stand near the soft old-leather settees and give a soothing touch.

The den at the back of the house is all unmistakably Duke's. It's as large as a small gymnasium and is almost an exact replica of the den he had in the ranch house at Encino. It houses Duke's unique collection of Civil War miniatures, paintings and rare sculptures by the western artist Charles Russell. There are nearly three hundred cups, shields, plaques and framed citations from his many films and his work for the Marine Corps too.

His Oscar from *True Grit* now holds pride of place on his huge
dark desk. Duke's collection of real Hopi Kachina Indian dolls
from Arizona, said to be one of the best collections in the world,
stands dimly-lit on their own shelf.

The remark made by one of their friends, an antiques expert,
when he visited their home for the first time, sums it up well.
'You have a collection of early American folk-lore here that many
a museum would envy,' he said. 'And your oriental treasures
are the kind a New England sea captain would have brought
back from the China Trade.'

Duke's den also serves as the Waynes' private projection
room. The screen slides electrically up into the roof when not
in use. One of their favourite ways of entertaining friends is to
show them the latest films – *before* they go out on release.

'We have a library of all Duke's films and he often laughs
at himself in some of them,' Pilar told me. 'He is a lot of fun
to watch when he's watching his own films. But some of his
remarks shouldn't go beyond our own four walls. My favourites
are *The Quiet Man, Sands Of Iwo Jima, The Alamo* because
I know just how much he put into it, and of course *True Grit*
in which he *really* showed everybody!'

Duke has a theory about his films, which may explain partly
why he's been at the top longer than any other actor. He feels
they appeal more to men than to women. He says as it's the
men who mostly take women to the movies, the film ought to
be about something that really appeals to a man.

'I know I could never get him to take me to a movie unless
he also wanted to see it,' say Pilar. 'Come to think of it, he
only ever took me out to one picture apart from premieres –
and that was *The Long Long Trailer* with Lucille Ball. And
I had to beg and beg. This was during our first two years of
marriage and I said to him "How is it you never go to see the
shows, when it's your whole business?" He thought a moment
then said "Yes, I should." Shortly after that he started building
our first projection room!'

Today, whenever the Waynes want to run new films for guests,
Pilar calls the studio who tell her what they have available.
She decides on a couple, then the studio sends the films over
with a projectionist to run them.

Both Duke and Pilar have fundamental, conservative tastes

in movies, Naturally they don't always know what the new film will be like and occasionally this has led to awkward moments at their soirées.

'I hate having a group of friends over to the house and run a film and then find everyone is embarrassed about it,' says Pilar. 'Twice I've told the projectionist to stop the film and take it away. We saw *Rosemary's Baby* here and I thought some of the scenes were really embarrassing. During the rape scene I'd had enough and I stood up and said "Stop it and get it out of here." My guests must have thought I was some kind of purity princess but I couldn't help it. Films like that make me and many other people feel terrible. They get up afterwards and are sad and morose for a long time.

'I like a film which gives me something, takes me away and makes me forget about the dreary routine things or the nasty side of life. I like to be uplifted, films that make me laugh or feel better, more compassionate or more inspired. I don't want to sit and watch filth, even clever filth. Duke gets quite violent about this sort of thing himself. Years ago in love scenes they kissed and dissolved. Now you sit there and watch the whole thing, in some films almost the sexual act. I feel sorry for the young today who go to see these movies. What dreams can be left, what illusions are not shattered, what concepts of romance are left in their lives?

'I don't think we're naive for feeling this way, but we do feel some standards are worth preserving. It's important to be positive not negative, to be optimistic not pessimistic, to look for the best and finest and try for that, and not be satisfied with ugliness if there is beauty within your sight.'

This attitude, which is also felt by many people among modern movie audiences, is also shared by Duke himself. He feels there are too many films today that just set out to titillate the senses, which justify or glorify neuroses and psychoses of all kinds and are often mere excuses for talented pornography. He once put it very clearly in an open letter to a Hollywood trade paper.

'I've been in pictures all my life and I deplore the garbage now being flashed on the screen,' he wrote. 'It's giving the world a false, nasty impression of us. And it isn't doing our own people a lot of good either. I don't like to see Hollywood's

G

blood stream polluted with perversion and immoral or amoral nuances. Filthy minds, filthy words and filthy thoughts have no place in films, which I see as a universal instrument at once entertaining people and encouraging them to work towards a better, finer and freer world. Pictures are family entertainment and you just don't tell dirty stories to kids.'

Duke isn't, however, against specialized films for specialized audiences. He isn't a dreamer living in an ivory tower. His own speech is earthy enough, his own films are tough enough and right from the start his sexual authority with women was obvious. But he says 'I have no time for pseudo-sophisticates who belittle courage, honour and decency. I don't condemn healthy sex. Every picture should have some sex but not in a dirty way.' In his own life he champions a rugged, radical individualism, but he can certainly be classed a romantic.

After lung cancer laid him low Duke clearly wasn't going to cripple himself further by running from film to film like he'd been doing for the previous four years when trying to recover from his business setbacks. Also, apart from being busily occupied with the big move from Encino, he was working hard at rejuvenating Batjac, so he took on cameo roles for a time.

He played a small role with Kirk Douglas in *Cast A Giant Shadow*, about the formation of modern Israel. In one scene he had to leap from a jeep to wrestle with Douglas but he damaged a spinal disc in the fall. A quick visit to hospital, a couple of days taking it easy and Duke was back at work.

He was madder at the jeep than anything else. 'Hell, to get even with a horse after a fall you can get up and give it a swat in the rump,' he joked. 'But what can you do with a jeep? Pull off its tail pipe?'

In George Stevens' story of the life of Christ, *The Greatest Story Ever Told*, Duke played the Centurion at the foot of the Cross. But he rose above his unaccustomed surroundings to bring to his short role the dignity and authority now being expected of him.

In *Eldorado*, in which he was teamed with Robert Mitchum and his old colleague, director Howard Hawks, Duke's acting and screen persona began the upward surge that culminated in his flawless portrait of the flawed sheriff in *True Grit*.

In it he played an ageing gun fighter hired by ruthless range barons to protect their interests against the local settlers and their drunken sheriff. When Wayne finds out the true nature of the job and that the sheriff (Robert Mitchum) is an old acquaintance who once saved him from a lynch mob but has become a pathetic figure from the man he once was, Wayne transfers his loyalties and backs up Mitchum. The picture contained some fine knockabout comedy scenes and Wayne surpassed his performance as Sheriff T. Chance in *Rio Bravo*, a film *Eldorado* faintly resembled.

He made major changes in his appearance too. Howard Hawks talked him into forgoing Parker, the old 'hayburner' horse he'd used in many films, and into riding a mighty Appaloosa stallion instead. It was a superb looking animal, grey and white with black dots.

'You'll have to dress up a little when you ride this handsome fellow, Duke,' said Hawks. 'Otherwise nobody'll ever notice you.'

'Okay,' said Duke. 'I'll dress up.'

He got rid of the mousey double-breasted fireman's shirt he'd worn for years and wore one coloured bright orange. He also put a silver band round his stetson.

'How's this now?' he drawled. 'Do I look all right? I sure don't aim to be upstaged by my own horse!'

In *The War Wagon*, good performances plus the excellent combination of Wayne with Kirk Douglas again, raised the serio-comic western above the level of any normal horse opera. Duke was now in his sixtieth year but he still looked born to the saddle. With the supremacy his age and all the years of experience had invested him, the big man on the big horse was now a combination that added up to a powerful image indeed.

Writing about Wayne making this film, *Time* magazine noted 'In *The War Wagon* he mounted his horse with his own steam, while co-star Kirk Douglas, ten years younger, had to leap aboard with the help of an unseen trampoline.'

By now Duke had won through from his tough days in the early sixties and had master-minded his business interests into a more than healthy position. One estimate said Batjac had now diversified its holdings *outside* of motion pictures into a ten million dollar empire. Duke had no need to work in movies merely for the money and his earlier plans to concentrate more on producing and directing were revived.

He began work on *The Green Berets,* his most ambitious project since *The Alamo.* He bought the Robin Moore novel, negotiated with the US Defence Department for co-operation, scouted locations and starred in and directed the whole film himself. *The Green Berets* aroused controversy from start to finish. Two studios Wayne approached turned the project down but finally Warner-Seven Arts backed him. American liberals accused him of glorifying the 'unpopular' war in Viet Nam.

'Nonsense!' bellowed Wayne, a super patriot whose hawkish views and hatred of Communism are well known. 'These boys in the US Special Forces over there are doing the most dangerous work any soldiers have ever undertaken. They are highly trained espionage men trained in medics, demolition, communications, languages and psychological warfare. They patrol behind enemy lines and can only be protected from the air. I want to show the folk back home just what they're up against out there, their heroism against tremendous odds.

'Glorifying an unpopular war? What war was ever popular for God's sake? They don't want to be in Viet Nam any more than anyone else. I was out there and I went to several A camps and I talked to these boys. I tell you once you go over there you won't be middle-of-the-road. Bobby Kennedy and Fulbright and Eugene McCarthy and all those goddam "let's-be-sweet-to-our-enemies" guys, all they're doing is helping the Reds and hurting their own country.'

Duke knew what he was talking about. In July 1966, partly to get material for his film and partly as a goodwill trip to visit the troops ('I can't sing or dance but I can sure shake a lot of hands') he toured Marine outposts in Viet Nam. He got so far up front one day he heard the shots from Vietcong snipers' rifles.

'They were so far away,' he told reporters afterwards, 'I didn't stop signing autographs.' In fact the bullets tore up the ground only seventeen yards from him.

Duke celebrated his sixtieth birthday at the premiere of *The War Wagon* in Arlington, Texas. Two days later he started working without rest over the long Memorial Day weekend on his first location at Fort Benning, Georgia, for *The Green Berets.*

'I'd sooner make it right there in Viet Nam,' he said. 'But

if you started shooting off blanks over there they might shoot back with live ammo.'

For the best part of the next three months, everyone on the film, co-stars David Janssen, Aldo Ray, Jim Hutton and Bruce Cabot included, knew big Duke Wayne was back in charge. Leathery, cussing and hollering phrases like 'Get that camera over here and shut the hell up!' he stamped about in the dust, his green beret at a rakish angle, bawling orders through a portable mike, scribbling script changes, charging about in his own scenes and directing all the others. Now and again he listened to the odd suggestion from veteran director Mervyn Le Roy, whom Warner-Seven Arts had sent out to help speed up the schedule. (This irritated Duke but being an old friend of Le Roy's, he didn't embarrass him by taking any action.) But there was no doubt about who was running the show.

There's no doubt either that Wayne can push people around if he needs to. The authority that comes over on the screen is there in real life. Major Jerold R. Dodds, a real life Green Beret whom the Pentagon delegated to be technical adviser on the film, watched big Duke in action, shook his head and told me 'I'll tell you one thing. If I'm in half the shape he's in when I'm his age I'll be happy. He's a fantastic man. And his leadership qualities are real.'

Wayne has a tough sense of humour too which helps keep people on their toes. When the film transferred to the back lot at Warners in Hollywood for final shooting, I watched Duke direct a scene where US Army Captain William Olds, playing a downed pilot in the jungle, had to be jerked off the ground and fifty feet into the air to simulate a spectacular helicopter air rescue.

It was a dangerous stunt in which an untrained man could get his neck broken. And it involved the use of a giant crane, an electric winch and a system of slip ropes.

Everything was set. Duke shouted 'Action!' and Captain Olds shot high into the air as if fired from a cannon. As the slip ropes let him down again gently, his face broke into a smile of relief that everything had worked okay.

'Right,' said Duke, clapping his hands with a straight face. 'Now let's have some film in that camera this time!' Only his quick wink told Olds he was joshing.

By and large the critics took *The Green Berets* to be representative of Wayne's personal hawkish views on Viet Nam and attacked it. New York Congressman Benjamin S. Rosenthal accused Wayne and the Army of conspiracy. 'The movie,' Rosenthal claimed, 'has become a useful and skilled device employed by the Pentagon to present a view of the war which was disputed in 1967 and is largely repudiated today.'

The picture, however, was a huge smash at the box office and Wayne leaped again into the battle. '*Green Berets* made eight million dollars in the first three months of its release. And that's what it cost. From then on we moved into profits. This so-called intellectual group aren't in touch with the American people,' he said, referring to the liberal 'doves' who wanted to withdraw from Viet Nam and the would-be appeasers of the Communists. 'In spite of them, the American people don't feel that way. Instead of taking a census they ought to count the tickets that we sold to that picture.'

Whether Wayne was right in surmising because many people went to see his movie it meant they supported the war in Viet Nam is a target for obvious argument, but later Duke was more explicit to me about his own personal interest.

'I made that picture primarily for entertainment value. If I was going to work that hard to get over a point of view, I'd state my opinions rather than try to do it in a piece of entertainment. I don't think pictures are meant for messages. I think they can emotionally affect people which in turn may affect thinking, but this picture was made strictly for entertainment and to show what those lads are going through.'

Wayne does believe America is right in trying to check the advance of Communism in south-east Asia. But his political views are referred to later.

In early 1968 Duke put himself back under the direction of young Andy McLaglen when he starred in *The Hellfighters*, playing a part based on the life of Texan 'Red' Adair, who won fame and became a millionaire for his ability to put out oil field fires. (Adair was also the man who plugged the North Sea gas leak off Britain's coast.) The film explored the personal and professional problems that beset a father and son who earn their livings extinguishing oil field flare-ups.

Five one hundred and twenty-five foot fire jets were devised by special effects men for the most dangerous scenes and when it was time for him to get among them, Duke said 'I'll only go if Red tells me it's safe!'

Adair, who was technical adviser on the film, said it was okay. And Duke, protected by a metal shield and a constant spray of water to stop him from getting burned, moved in.

As he came out he cracked. 'I'll never steam a clam again!' But he wasn't complaining. By now he was getting a million dollars per picture, plus ten per cent of the gross.

It was before he completed that movie that Duke first read the galley proofs of Charles Portis' new novel *True Grit*. He knew instantly that the book would become a nationwide best seller and that the character of the US Marshal Rooster Cogburn would give him his best role in years. He felt the same kind of excitement he'd felt when Jack Ford had first handed him the story for *Stagecoach* nearly thirty years earlier.

'Rooster was the kind of Marshal the screen had never seen before,' said Duke. 'An old sloppy-looking, hard-drinking, disreputable, one-eyed son of a blank who'd been around long enough to know for sure you don't mess around with outlaws, but use every trick in the book, fair or foul, to bring 'em to justice.

'In Rooster's world a kick in the face was clean fighting, especially if it was a struggle for life. He brought his prisoners back alive – unless they got ideas. But they came back anyway – dead and slung over the backside of a horse.'

He liked Rooster so much he tried to buy the movie rights and make the film for Batjac. But producer Hal Wallis beat him to the bank. Duke didn't give up – he chased after the part alone.

'I think it is rather like me,' Duke told Hollywood writer Wayne Warga at the time. 'Of course it could have been Lee Marvin but he might have made it too theatrical. I can get away with a little theatricality because I seldom use it. Rooster Cogburn is a mean old bastard and that's me! I played it very faithful to the book.'

Duke played it like no one else could have played it. From the veteran members of the crew, many of whom had worked with Wayne for years, to the director himself, Henry Hathaway again, few were in any doubt as they watched him go through his scenes in Colorado with a rare lusty enjoyment that Duke was on his way to an Oscar nomination – if not the Oscar itself.

'It was a real challenge to me,' Duke told me later, 'because it had a style of dialogue I wasn't used to and it put me to the test. When the kids and widow were in danger, Rooster was drunk but when it was time to get the job done he was right there. It gave me more than in many movies an opportunity to spread myself.'

But Duke wasn't counting his chickens. He hadn't worked for an Oscar but once it was within his reach he wanted it, no doubt about it. He'd missed it narrowly twice – once when nominated for *Sands Of Iwo Jima* and once when he'd been in the running for a nomination for his role in *She Wore A Yellow Ribbon.* Now after some forty years as an actor, it would be like a final accolade, the cream on the top of his Irish coffee. A proof too perhaps that he had a lot more going for him than mere popularity.

But he didn't waste time hanging around resting on his laurels. He plunged back into work as an ex-Union Cavalry officer rounding up wild horses for a living in 20th Century Fox's Maximilian era shoot-up *The Undefeated,* in which he co-starred with Rock Hudson.

It was a picture that seemed jinxed from start to finish for Duke. Early on in Mexico, during a festive evening with some of the cast and crew, Duke sat down too darn heavily in an old chair. Mexican chairs are made for little Mexicans of around a hundred and forty pounds and when Duke's two hundred and forty-four descended upon it, it collapsed and Duke ended up on the hard tile floor with a couple of fractured ribs. It was a pretty silly way to get injured for a man who's done the dangerous stunts Duke has, but they just shot round him a few days and then Duke went back to work.

A few weeks later while doing the location scenes at Baton Rouge, Louisiana, a stirrup broke suddenly on his cantering horse and down Duke went – ploughing a rather deep furrow in the Louisiana soil with his right shoulder 'I sure damaged that pasture,' he quipped, trying to hide the pain. It was the same shoulder he'd torn during his football days but though the injury was bad enough to trouble him for weeks, he got straight back on his horse and finished the scene.

After *The Undefeated,* Duke and Pilar went away on their first two month holiday together for years. A cruise on *The Wild Goose* first, then they spent the rest of the time at Duke's cattle ranch in Springerville, Arizona.

Duke's Oscar nomination as best actor came through while he was winding up *Chisum,* which was again directed by Andy McLaglen.

He was happily surprised but up against Richard Burton's performance in *Anne Of The Thousand Days* and Peter O'Toole's magnificent portrayal of Henry II in *The Lion In Winter,* he didn't feel he had much chance. He had never been a critics' actor. But he didn't become defensive about it. When asked how he felt about the possibility of winning the Oscar at last, Duke was courteous but refrained from his comment of earlier years when asked about awards: 'You can't eat awards. Nor, more to the point, drink 'em.'

On the glittering Academy Awards night Duke was one of the celebrity comperes himself, working as the star-studded occasion was bounced off the satellite and beamed to TV sets all over the world, to help the image of the Hollywood he loves.

Later, as he sat with Pilar among the other stars and Barbra Streisand went through the ritual of announcing the Best Actor nominees, Duke admits he started feeling 'all gooey inside. For the first time in my life I was scared. I was quaking in my boots.'

When Barbra opened the envelope and announced his name as the winner he felt a brief moment of panic, but after a quick squeeze from Pilar's hand he went up on stage with that familiar loping walk and in a short acceptance speech he clutched the golden statue and said 'I thought some day I might get some award for lasting so long! But I never thought I would get this particular award.'

That night the viewing world of millions saw something they'd never seen before. Big John Wayne had tears in his eyes.

9

THE STAR AND THE MAN

I've many times heard it said that John Wayne doesn't *act*, he just plays himself in film after film.

Anyone naive enough to believe any actor could stay at the very peak of such a ruthless profession and become the biggest box office draw the world has ever known – or conceivably ever will know – merely by being himself, needs his brains examining.

Duke became an actor by accident. Luck got him in all right, but it was work that kept him going up that hard slogging real-life trail to the top. It's all very well to say men like Jack Ford and Howard Hawks gave him chances. The question is why? Duke's stamina is legendary. His talent was acquired, honed on the hard grindstone of experience.

Few people know it but before *Stagecoach* in 1939, he had made a hundred and thirty films. They were mostly those pretty dreadful B western quickies and serials which he made for some ten years before *Stagecoach*, but as he says 'I worked like the very devil.' Once he made a fifteen-chapter serial in eighteen days.

Right from the start he hated anything unreal or phoney. When he was made the screen's first singing cowboy he soon turned it in. It wasn't *his* voice and *he* wasn't playing the guitar. Not only did he, with top stunt man Yakima Canutt, invent the bar room brawling technique still used in films today but he was the first screen hero to hurl chairs, vases and tables *back* at the villains. 'If the heavies can throw furniture at me, why can't I throw it back?' he argued. 'Why does a cowboy star have to be so stupidly noble he can't give as good as he gets?'

Wayne's acting credo has frequently been reported in the taut but over-simplified phrase 'I don't act, I react.' But there's more to it than that. In these days when many of the new young stars

Duke in *True Grit* ready for the big fight

Left
Henry Hathaway rehearses a
scene with Duke Wayne and Glenn
Campbell in *True Grit*. 'Hank' and
Duke are old colleagues and it is
fitting that Hank, over seventy,
should be the director who helped
Duke to his first Oscar

Duke on location for *The Undefeated*

Duke with his youngest child Marisa
(born February 1966) in the garden of
their beautiful home at Newport
Beach, California

Left
Duke at sixty-two lashes out a right
hander in true John Wayne style at
Rock Hudson in *The Undefeated*.
On this film Duke fractured two ribs
when an old Mexican chair collapsed
beneath him, and a few weeks later
he dislocated his shoulder in a fall
from a horse. But he carried on with
his scenes so as not to hold up the
film

Overleaf
Duke and his wife Pilar

go in for that mannered 'Method' style of acting, so consciously real it's still somehow unreal, Duke's views on acting are perhaps pertinent.

'There can only be one boss on the set and that's the director,' he says. 'You are really just paint as an actor. If a director uses your colour well, that's fine. The difference between good acting and bad acting is the difference between acting and reacting. In a bad picture you can see them acting all over the place. But in a good one they *re*act in a logical natural way to the situations they're in, so the audience can identify with them. I figure one look that works is better than twenty lines of dialogue. If a script calls for something I believe is foreign to the character's nature, I simply say "I'm too limited to put that across. I'm not that good an actor." I never try to go low on integrity and I'll never do anything that will humiliate a man in the audience.'

The top stars of the day who appeared in Duke's early films were pleased to find themselves with an actor who never tried to upstage them. He was often the passenger in a situation instead of assuming the dynamic, active role. While the other actors went on to ham it up, Duke just took it all in his stride, usually winning the sympathy of the audience. Whereas Clark Gable was always better when he forced the issue with a girl, Wayne scored when the girl made the running. His sexual authority was strong enough for him not to need to push it around.

In the early forties he was playing the rebellious, hard-drinking sons of the west who'd straighten out okay if they didn't get a bullet in the head first. By the late forties he had graduated to fatherhood, the tough Marine bullying a platoon of recruits to manhood, the foreman in the construction or oilfield camp, the lone rider on a horse who rode down from the mountains with a gutful of tough experience who led the settlers against the Indians, the ruthless range barons or whatever.

Always he was the typical good man with the courage to kill if he had to in his fight against injustice and if the killer were evil. He feared no man but was kind and reserved with women.

In the fifties, from *Red River* onwards, he began to play the respected veteran roles, ageing Cavalry officers, ranchers, die-hards, lawmen – men of dignity and often tragic loneliness, but men who could still do what they had to do if pushed. His acting began to gain an unmistakable authority. He was beginning to be able to characterize the essence of the American soul which D. H. Lawrence once described as 'harsh, isolate, stoic and a killer'.

Here too began the mature quality which characterized his relationships with his screen lovers and wives. You never saw Wayne involved in hysterical argument, long, lascivious kissing scenes or groping with women's clothes. His passion was a reserved yet powerful thing, powerful *because* it was reserved.

Maureen O'Hara who played his screen wife in several films tells an interesting anecdote about what it's like as a woman to act with Wayne. During a scene in *McLintock!* Duke told Maureen he didn't like the way she was playing it.

He said angrily 'Come on Maureen, get going. This is your scene.'

Maureen said she was trying to go fifty fifty.

'Fifty fifty, hell!' said Duke. 'It's *your* scene so take it.' Then he added under his breath 'If you can!'

Duke vets his scripts carefully for unreal dialogue and situations and for character clues. When he was playing the naval Captain promoted to Admiral in *In Harm's Way* in Honolulu, he told British columnist David Lewin:

'In this picture I must show that I care about the other people otherwise when they go off and get killed on my orders people would hate me. I don't mind audiences hating me, they did perhaps in *Red River*, but they understood my point of view.

'Kirk Douglas in this film has a rape scene with a girl who is engaged to another man. Douglas gets killed in action. Now if I were playing his part I would want the girl's boy friend to return, and face me, and kill me. I don't mind dying in a film if the confrontation is direct. My father used to tell me "If you tell a lie, admit it." I have always believed that. I always believe in facing everything directly. If you are doing corn, face it straight and don't fool around with it trying to make it something else. It is still just corn.'

This kind of honesty is what has always made people believe in Wayne's sincerity.

Now, in the seventies, in the normally climacteric time in

an actor's life, Duke's belt bites into his girth, though there's still plenty of muscle beneath the avoirdupois. He has to diet these days because since his operation he's unable to exercise as much as he would like. His hands are like aged bark, his face ravined and scored by lightning, his neck still size 18. At a time when most star actors' screen lives are drawing to a close he turned in his Oscar winning performance in *True Grit*. It was a part that seemed to many a subtle parody of his own earlier heroic roles, though Duke himself denies it.

There's no doubt that Wayne's own pioneer heritage and emotional strength have played a great part in his development as an actor. Most of his films have glorified the kind of courage and indomitable spirit which sent his Scots and Irish ancestors west to help create from a harsh wilderness the prosperous and democratic civilization America first became. It's partly because he epitomised these basic early national virtues that he has become an internationally popular star.

No one would pretend all Duke's films have been good ones. Some of them, he readily admits, have been little short of terrible. But to me people who dismiss his work as a whole seem basically vacuous snobs who today, in their slick, soft and affluent world, disdain the courage and earthiness of the men – most of them from the Old Country – who gave America its first backbone.

Wayne is strongly moral in outlook when it comes to the influence his films might have upon the young, especially in sexual matters. 'No one in any of my films will ever be served drinks by a girl with no top to her dress,' he said once. He deplores too the glorification of the psychotic weakling which occurs in some modern films. 'I'd never play that kind of part myself,' he says.

To have such attitudes one minute and then to depict screen violence with gun and fist the next, may seem paradoxical. But Wayne denies his films are violent in any corrupting sense.

'The characters are usually rather likeable,' he says. 'Fights with too much violence are dull. The violence in my pictures is lusty and a little bit humorous because I believe humour nullifies violence.'

For a powerful man whose screen image is one of unconquerable toughness, Wayne is extraordinarily gentle off screen.

His wife describes him as 'one of nature's gentlemen'. When I visited him during the making of *The Undefeated* in Louisiana he'd just damaged his shoulder in that fall from his horse and he was standing around in a heat of 102 degrees in the shade, waiting his turn to walk into a shot. He was surrounded by gawping fans who'd gate-crashed the location, nasal-voiced matrons dressed in atrocious colours, pimply young men showing off in front of their girl friends, people who mistook him for someone else. He posed endlessly for their box cameras, offset the irritating effrontery of a man who half-pushed him between two girls by saying 'Sure. I don't mind if the girls don't!' and smilingly put up with tactless remarks that bordered upon insult.

'I don't mind,' he told me later with a grin. 'They get so confused they don't know what they're saying half the time. I love 'em all.'

One of the occupational hazards of being a star with a tough guy image is that in places like public bars drunks tend to pick on you – to test if you're as tough as you appear on screen.

'No one's as tough as he appears on screen,' admits Duke. 'A film fight is the opposite of a real fight because the camera has to see everything. You have to reach way back and sock out and make a big show. In a real fight you hit short and close.' But Wayne has had his share of trouble from men who wanted to prove themselves, especially during his younger days.

His stock answer to men who wanted to fight him in bars was 'Sure, but let me buy you a drink first.' Invariably the man would join him for a drink, Duke would explain he wasn't nearly as tough in real life as he was in films, and the trouble would be averted. Also he could outdrink most men.

'I didn't mind them showing off in front of their girl friends, just so long as they didn't push me too far and make me out to be too yellow-bellied!' he says.

Getting Wayne to talk about any real life fights is virtually impossible. 'Oh, they don't bother me any more,' he says, playing it down. 'They accept me now. I'm older and I've become part of the family. But I never belted anyone in public. Oh, I took a couple of guys outside once and clipped them down to size, but I never did it public. That was the golden rule –

never do it where it will help their egos!' And that's all he would say.

I happen to know of one man, however, whom Wayne did more than clip down to size. He was a film executive, a big tough fellow who'd done a spot of prize fighting. He didn't like Duke and one day he started riding him hard. Duke took it as long as he could but when the man put up his fists, Duke slung a right that must have felt like a felled telephone pole. The man went to hospital with a fractured jaw. The event was hushed up at the time.

Later, when the man recovered, he said ruefully. 'I guess it was my fault. I thought for a long time I could take Duke Wayne. Now I *know* I can't!'

Ralph Volkie, who has been Duke's trainer for sixteen years and has trained five ring champions in his time, once said 'Duke's got the hardest right hand punch of any man I've ever seen, including Dempsey, and I've seen 'em all.'

The late James Edward Grant, scriptwriter for many of Duke's films, once told a story of what happened one night years ago when they were filming in Santa Fé, New Mexico.

'Duke let a stranger horn in on one of our private parties. Later I saw this guy in a bar displaying a bandaged hand and proclaiming how he'd knocked Wayne out cold. I hurried back to our hotel and found Duke, quite unbattered, peacefully asleep. I woke him up and told him the story. Duke laughed and rolled over in bed. Ten minutes later he sat up and started pulling on his clothes. "Where was that guy", he wanted to know, so I told him.

'The stranger was still at the bar. Duke walked in, grabbed him by the collar and hoisted him off the floor. "Did you have a fight with me tonight?" he asked. "N . . . No sir," stammered the guy. Duke held him up a few seconds more then dropped him to the floor. "Okay," he said and stalked out again.'

Today that wouldn't happen, nor anything like it. Duke wouldn't get involved at all. Much of the violence has been drained out of him and a man who has faced down death by cancer can have nothing to gain by facing down a stranger in a bar.

In her sixteen years of marriage to Duke, Pilar says she can only remember one tiff – way back in 1956 shortly after their first home caught fire and nearly burned down and they rented a house while it was being repaired.

'I can't remember what it was all about now,' she told me. 'But sometimes when he'd been away on a long location, it took us a few days to get adjusted again as for several weeks our lives and surroundings had been quite different. We were moving into a rented house while ours was being redecorated and modernized and that's when the row occurred. But we knew we loved each other too much to ever separate. He *can* get mad but he's always over it very quickly and it's all forgotten. To tell the truth, I've never known him harbour a grudge or a petty thought or say anything denigrating about anyone.'

All of this helps explain why Duke is so highly respected in his profession. If he wasn't called Duke already Hollywood would almost certainly by now have dubbed him 'The King' because there is no one else better fitted to pick up the crown dropped by the late Clark Gable.

There is no doubt however that Wayne's intransigent Right wing views, his hawkish stand on Viet Nam and his apolitical statements that stem from his almost paranoic hatred of Communism, have helped make him many enemies in Hollywood.

Much has been made of the fact that in 1949 he became President of the Motion Picture Alliance for the Preservation of American Ideals, a Rightist organization dedicated to run all Communists or men with Communist leanings out of the film industry. (Robert Taylor was President before him and Ward Bond after him). The Alliance was generally credited with giving the House Un-American Activities Committee the names of all suspected Hollywood Reds and playing a part which resulted in the jailing of the 'Hollywood Ten' for contempt. These men, some of them top talents, were virtually blackballed from working in the industry and some didn't get to work in Hollywood again for almost ten years.

Although Duke was a prime mover in the Alliance, he wasn't as Right wing as many of its members. One group believed Once a Communist, always a Communist', but Wayne didn't go that far. In many circles the feeling persisted that Wayne who *is* a super patriot, was being 'used' and that it took considerable prodding to make him join the vigilantes in their hunt for Reds. In fact at one Alliance meeting Duke publicly

forgave actor Larry Parks for admitting his old Leftist indis-
cretions in the thirties – but he was rewarded with a sizzling
blast from columnist Hedda Hopper, who reminded him of
America's boys dying in Korea.

Wayne as a political animal is not easy to assess. He once
said he considers politics a 'necessary evil'. He is sometimes
accused of being politically naive – a condition if true that he
shares with probably ninety per cent of the American popu-
lation.

One American writer wrote 'Duke sees America as a big white
colonial home with an expanse of green lawn and a high picket
fence. The Communists are the termites gnawing away in the
basement and when insects are trying to destroy your home, you
call in the exterminator. His feeling for rugged American individualism is more emotional than ideological, and more gutsy
than intellectual.'

Wayne certainly loves his country with enormous idealized
passion. His fundamentalist nature basically sees the world as
an arena of conflict between absolute good and absolute evil,
and he feels a man should scorn compromise, tolerate no ambi-
guities. He dislikes the so-called 'Permissive Society' with its
confusing of standards and its attendant amorality.

During the Republican national convention at Miami Beach
in the summer of 1968, Duke turned up and gave the assembly
a pep talk on super nationalism.

'To use a good old American expression, I think this is the
party that gives a damn,' he said. As the delegates shouted
their approval, he went on to say America was more than laws
and government. It was an outlook. He recalled what he said
when Dean Martin had asked him what he wanted for his
daughter. 'I told him I wanted her to be as grateful as I am.
Grateful for every day of my life I wake up in the United
States of America.' He said he would teach her the Lord's
Prayer and some of the Psalms. 'I don't care if she never
memorizes the Gettysburg address but I hope she understands it.'

It was all simple patriotic stuff like that but it went over
well and one writer commented it was perhaps a good thing
Wayne wasn't running for President.

During the Presidential elections that year, George Wallace
asked him to run as his vice-presidential candidate. But Wayne

refused. 'Mr Wallace has some good ideas but I'm certainly not a backer of his,' he said, then added 'I would never go into politics myself. I only get mixed up in them to help voice the other side.'

When I was talking to Duke on the location for *The Undefeated* he was waiting for the cameras to be set up for a cavalry charge, when suddenly a man came up to him with a message from the local Republican party asking Duke to go along and say a few words.

'Oh, heck,' he groaned. 'I just don't have the time. I'm not a goddam politician. If I was I'd sure be a good deal further ahead in this business than I am! But they are perhaps a necessary evil.'

I asked him why then did he get embroiled in public political discussion, and why he visited war fronts and why he supported American intervention in Viet Nam?

It was a complicated question to ask anyone, never mind an actor in between shots on a hot dusty location waiting for the director to call him for more filming but Duke didn't hesitate.

'You know, I just think this is my country, the country that I love,' he replied. 'And I get mad these days when I see our boys out there getting killed and maimed and the people back home aren't behind them. I can't figure out why these days we're always pulling ourselves down and kow-towing to everyone else. However the world views us, we are reaching the point where further appeasement might well mean disaster. This isn't what made us a great nation.

'When I made *The Green Berets* the liberals, or so-called liberals, said I was trying to glorify an unpopular war. What war was ever popular? I said. And it's no argument to say we are miles from home and on foreign territory in our efforts to contain Communism. We were on foreign territory too when we joined Britain to push back Hitler and crush the evil of Nazism. If we hadn't done that where would these liberals be today? In gas chambers?

'It was perfectly all right when we were pushing Hitler back. Does anyone believe after the Stalin purges, the labour camps, the repression of free expression, opinion or artistry, the jailing of brilliant writers, that Communism – either Russian or Chinese – with its enslavement and stifling of liberty and individual freedom – is any *lesser* an evil?'

Wayne stamped his big boot in the dust as if to emphasize his points. He seemed to have suddenly stepped right out of the John Wayne character as he revealed something of the patriotism that underlines his beliefs.

'We had a right to be in Viet Nam. The people were being tortured. What little leadership they had was getting murdered or kidnapped. Our liberals say we should walk out, not back the South Viet Nam government, yet they came up with a form of constitutional government during a war when they were hard pressed and were the underdogs. It took the colonies of the United States eleven years after our little set-to with England before we could come up with anything all thirteen colonies would sign. Yet these people managed to do it during a war. I don't know what the liberals expect these poor people to do if we leave. I can't figure it out. We fought in Germany because of what they were doing to the Jews and to freedom and as far as I'm concerned this is the same sort of thing. As far as I'm concerned the Communists are our enemy, not the Russian or Chinese people, but the Communist conspiracy *is* our enemy.'

But didn't he feel the continued war in south east Asia must eventually escalate into a third world war?

'The only way Viet Nam could bring on a third world war is if Russia figures she can't win the world any other way. What the hell – they're gradually taking over weaker nations, pushing their leaders out of windows, and finally crushing them when they try to win their own freedom, like in Hungary. *That* should have started a third world war. We'd been telling the people of oppressed nations "Stand up for your rights and we'll back you up." We've been doing this for years and now, suddenly it's a terrible thing we are keeping our word to the people of Viet Nam and south east Asia.'

The whole subject clearly made Duke's blood boil, but I asked him what he felt about young people, in both America and Britain, protesting against the Viet Nam war?

'I don't blame the kids for protesting, for their restlessness,' he said. 'Ideally they're right, of course. But I wish to hell they knew more about Communism than just its theories. I wish they knew its reality. And when I see some of them carrying the Vietcong flag on demonstrations I could – never mind. But we have to act *now*. Many people seem to stupidly think by just not doing anything, it will go away. It won't. And then we'll have another Dark Age.'

It seemed bizarre then, after Wayne's heated words, to watch him mount his horse, a big tough lovely old man with one lung gone and a busted shoulder, and do what must have been something near his thousandth cavalry charge. It wasn't right the first time so with a resigned grimace that turned into a grin, he went back another two hundred yards and did it again.

Was he right emotionally, wrong ideologically? One realizes that his conversation was straight off the cuff, with no pause for consideration or to find more exact careful ways of putting things. Besides, I have no wish to judge the man's politics. I watched him work, thundering up and down on his horse in that scorching heat. All the other riders were about half his age.

Right or wrong, a man could still learn a lot from him, I thought.

10

HOME FROM THE RANGE

It was early evening in the Wayne home. Pilar had just tucked her two youngest children safely up in bed and now she sat gratefully on the sofa in the main room for a brief rest. In the next room Aissa was struggling with her home work.

As the setting sun turned her view of Newport harbour a limpid rose colour, Pilar found herself wondering how Duke was getting along out on location in Louisiana. It really had been one of those 'jinx' pictures, she reflected. First Duke had fractured those two ribs, then he'd injured his weak shoulder again in that fall from his horse. She hoped nothing more would go wrong.

Just then the door opened and the Waynes' manservant Fausto came in to tell her Duke was on the phone. Worried about what might have happened now, she took the phone anxiously, only to hear Duke say from some two thousand miles away:

'Hi Pilar, now about this cheese soufflé – I've just highly whipped the eggs. What do I do now?'

She laughed then with relief and reminded Duke she had given him the recipe and exact instructions to take with him.

'Yeah,' he said sheepishly. 'But I lost it. I'm sorry.' He called twice more that night to get additional instructions. The fact that the phone calls cost maybe twenty times as much as the food he was cooking didn't bother Duke. He calls Pilar nearly every day he's away on location anyway.

'It's typical of his generous nature,' she says. 'He really is generous to a fault with his money. I can't walk past a store with him and say "Oh, I like that" because next day it arrives! I can't say I exactly help keep the purse strings tight either. We

117

both spend like crazy.' One recent Christmas he gave her *two* fur coats – a sable and a lynx.

Cooking on location for his retainers like Ralph, his trainer, and Dave, his make-up man, and other buddies in the crew, is Duke's latest hobby. He started it some five years ago. Before he goes away now he asks Pilar for several recipes of his favourite dishes. One is the chile cheese soufflé. Another is made from a corn and bran mixture called Hominy grits. This is a staple food in the deep South, a rather unpalatable grist food which, like Hawaiian *poi,* is mostly useful for absorbing grease from fatty meats like pork. But with chiles and a special meat sauce, Duke has found a way to make it very tasty. He also has three good casserole recipes. And losing them, as he frequently does, gives him good excuses to call Pilar.

Duke's films have grossed more at the box office than those of any star in history – more than two hundred million pounds to date – yet he remains basically a man of unaffected tastes. He could happily eat simple meat and potato meals every day. The only trouble is that now, with one lung removed, he can't exercise as much as he used to and he has to watch his weight as he is still a hearty eater. At home, salads are frequently on the menu.

Duke is a doting father and rather tends to spoil his children, especially when they are babies.

'When Aissa was a baby he spoilt her terribly,' Pilar admits. 'She used to do a little cha cha dance for him which sent him into howls of laughter. Every time he came back from trips he overloaded himself with stuffed dogs and teddy bears. Now he's doing the same thing with little Marisa. She can't do a thing wrong in her father's eyes right now!'

Duke is away filming so much that he feels he's more entitled to indulge the kids when he's home than Pilar. 'I'm sorry you can't spoil them,' he says. 'Someone has to be the disciplinarian. I'm afraid you'll have to be the villain of the piece.'

When he's back home Duke likes to stay home. He detests Hollywood parties. If he does go to one it has to be to someone's he and Pilar really like.

'Sometimes he'll go to a strange party if I really beg him and convince him it will be fun,' says Pilar. 'Then he'll say "All right, to please you we'll go." But he's far from being a recluse.'

In the early years at Encino the Waynes often had Jack Ford, Ward Bond and their wives and other friends over to the house. The conversation sparkled, the spirits flowed freely and often Pilar's sides ached from the hilarious stories they told about each other and other colleagues in Duke's rough action movies. Casual conversation around Wayne is often redolent of a college changing room, oddly youthful.

Today many of Duke's friends from the early days are no longer alive yet guests at their home frequently include the children of Duke's former buddies who are themselves now mostly in their forties. One of the Duke's mottoes is that a man should work hard at what he believes and play hard too – but never to the inconvenience of anyone else. Few men have played harder than Duke in his younger days and as for work – not only has he outlived most of the greats with whom he came up, like Clark Gable, Humphrey Bogart, Gary Cooper or Spencer Tracy to name but four, but he is today still way ahead at the top and working with the children of many of his contemporaries – and working them off their feet at that.

Today the Waynes' home life is slighly more staid than it used to be. It's certainly peaceful and content. Often Duke and Pilar just play bridge, poker or gin rummy. They owe each other thousands of dollars of course but neither ever pays up!

Duke is an incurable romantic, Pilar claims. 'If he's watching TV and something sad comes on he can cry like a baby. Some time back when some very good friends of ours, actress Claire Trevor and her husband Milton Bren, came over to see Zeffirelli's *Romeo and Juliet* in our projection room, it was such a beautiful sad picture that we all just sat there and cried. And I think Duke's eyes were damper than mine.'

One quality Duke has – a quality that the late Sir Winston Churchill also possessed – is that he finds it easy to relax with cat naps.

'He used to be a restless sleeper once but not these days,' says Pilar. 'He can just put his head on the pillow and go out like a switched-off light if he wants to. Sometimes he'll come home from the studios and say "We have to go out for dinner tonight, do we? Okay, I'd better grab ten minutes sleep." And off he goes – to wake up exactly ten minutes later. It's a wonderful capacity.'

For a man with the large number of commitments Duke has, it is probably an invaluable quality. And one reason he rests easy these days must lie in the fact that although he went through a bad time financially in the early sixties when several of his businesses showed unhealthy signs, they are all now back under his control and thriving again.

The Waynes have a cattle ranch in Springerville, Arizona – the 26 Bar Ranch – in which Duke is in partnership with Louis Johnson, an expert rancher. The ranch is fully automated and they have twenty thousand head of cattle in grass feeding and another twenty thousand in special finish feeding. Some forty thousand head go through the ranch each year. The herd is pure bred and last year Duke sold two bulls for thirty-five thousand dollars each. This year he sold four hundred thousand dollars worth on the hoof.

The whole Wayne family goes out for the big cattle sale each year and afterwards they hold a big party for all the cattle folk who visit Arizona from all over America. Duke and Pilar entertain them for three whole days, with barbecues and rodeos and those three days are really looked forward to by the family, especially by the kids.

Duke also has three thousand five hundred acres of cotton in Arizona plus the Red River Land Company, which administers some nineteen thousand irrigated acres in Stanfield. Recently he acquired mining concessions for forty-five thousand square miles in Nigeria, with some exploration rights on the Congo. He has a major interest in the Sea Service Corporation which supplies oil for yachts. And he owns an executive air company with two helicopters and his own Navaho jet plane, which are all kept at Orange County airport near their home.

These are all highly efficient well run businesses. The plane and helicopters are all chartered out when the Waynes aren't using them. The Navaho is a luxury turbo-prop jet which seats five and they use it occasionally to go skiing up in Sun Valley, Idaho, or at Aspen in Colorado.

In bad weather Duke has to drive to the studios to work but on most days he takes one of the helicopters as it saves so much time. He has to get up at 6 am every day he's filming and after a hard day's action shooting he doesn't feel much like driving sixty miles down the freeway each night to get home. This in spite of the fact that his car is like something out of science fiction. Duke got his car when he wrote to the boss of General Motors and said he wanted a custom-built car that would hold his six feet four inches, stetson and all.

I'll never forget my embarrassment when Pilar wanted to take me over to see Duke's yacht, *The Wild Goose,* and we decided to drive in Duke's car. In the garage it looked like a standard Pontiac station wagon. Then we got inside. There were so many instruments and dials I couldn't find out how to start the thing, never mind drive it! In the end Fausto had to drive us.

All this may sound as if Wayne is a really rich man. It depends what you mean by really rich. Certainly there *are* richer men than Duke in Hollywood. Bob Hope for instance, and director Henry Hathaway, who in his spare time is a brilliant financier, are but two. Perhaps Sinatra is another. But in terms of his family, his friends and the experiences of his life, Duke is certainly a rich man emotionally. As Pilar points out, it's difficult for a man like Wayne to be really rich in the material sense by the time he's finished paying his taxes.

'I smile when I hear him talking sometimes,' she says. 'He says "This is going to cost six million and that is going to cost three million," then I come home next day with a new dress and he says "What? It cost *that* much?" Not that he ever objects of course. Duke works very hard and is paid a lot but he hands out a great deal to Uncle Sam.'

When one talks to Pilar she is so vitally enthusiastic she makes life with Duke sound like one long idyll. Not that she intends to give that impression. But once when we were alone I asked Duke how *he* thought Pilar had found married life with him, especially in the early days.

'Well, certainly Pilar found it a challenge to settle down with me,' he said frankly. 'It's been a challenge for her all along. Settling down in that old mansion at Encino, lonely when I wasn't there, meeting all my other children, my old friends around us all the time. But now we're at the beach it's given her an opportunity, through her *own* personality, to make a group of friends for herself, which is very healthy.'

Pilar says she likes her life at Newport so much that everywhere else she goes, even the exotic film locations with Duke seem unatractive by comparison and she can't wait to get back. Their neighbours are kind and they are friendly with most of them now, she says, and although Duke is a famous star he's not bothered by anyone.

'They stared at him a lot for the first six months but now he's become just the fellow next door. Once in a while someone will say "Oh, we have a boy in Wyoming who'd like your photograph," so Duke poses with them for it, but he doesn't mind that at all. If they or his fans stopped bothering him altogether he'd be far more worried.

'He likes to know what the neighbours are doing, what new equipment they've got next door. And he can sit down and talk to a total stranger for three hours and enjoy every moment. He likes to find out what makes people tick.'

Often when Duke gets home after finishing a picture, his hair and sideburns are too long for his taste. 'I can't wait to get a haircut,' he tells Pilar. 'This is driving me nuts.' So he drives off to the local barber's shop and gets it cut down again.

Pilar's current hobby is tennis. She plays every day and takes part in local tournaments, along with Aissa. She was playing once on a court near the beach when Duke came sailing past on his boat, wearing tennis shoes. He saw his wife and shouted 'Hey, let me try it.' He left the boat and played a set with her.

'I was surprised because he'd never played it before yet he played very well – good timing and almost perfect strokes. But he was a very good football player once and he's a superb dancer, so I suppose it was natural enough really. He could be a good player if he wanted to.'

Pilar, along with some women stars and the wives of other male stars, like Neile McQueen, Jeanne Martin and Janet Leigh, is an active worker for SHARE the Hollywood charity that looks after mentally retarded children. When she works on the auction committee she has to go round local traders and persuade them to part with objects like bicycles, tape recorders or radios which are all sold in wrapped packages at an auction party. Top stars go along, pay extraordinary prices without knowing what they're getting, and the funds go to the children.

'We have our backers who pay for everything, like Frank Sinatra, Dean Martin and of course Duke. *He* doesn't get off very lightly, I can tell you!'

After my last visit to Pilar Wayne and just before I left the house, I asked her if she could sum up in one phrase what it has meant to her being married to Duke Wayne. She thought a moment then smiled and said simply: 'I'm a little biased perhaps, but seventeen years of loving and living with a man like Duke somehow elevates the whole concept of manhood in my eyes.'

Duke and Pilar are now sharing with their young family the most golden days of their lives. I'm tempted to say that from now on it will be all easy coasting downhill for Duke – except that I believe some of his finest performances are yet to come.

Many have said his 1970 Oscar came as the final accolade to his career. It would be truer to say that it came as a vote of confidence from which he will be inspired to tackle even more challenging and varied parts. After forty-three years as an actor in which he became the most successful star of all time, Hollywood, which has often paid high tribute to the occasional brilliant performance of an actor who seldom repeated it, suddenly realized it had in its midst a man who loved his business with an unrequited passion, who had never indulged in runaway production, who had been vilified in some circles for political opinions often misinterpreted, and realized at last it was behind in its payments. Duke's performance in *True Grit* allowed them to repay something of that debt.

One has the feeling that perhaps Duke Wayne may just go on for ever. In *Rio Lobo,* his late 1970 film, he's still falling from horses into icy streams, knocking big men cold with single right-handers, beating bad men to the draw. You know now you're watching an older man but a very fast old man indeed! In *Rio Lobo* he teamed up yet again with Yakima Canutt, who directed all the second unit action work. Duke's co-stars are young Jorge Rivero and Christopher Mitchum, son of his old colleague, Robert Mitchum. Duke doesn't try to get the girls in the film but has plenty of caustic remarks for young Rivero who *does.* Two of the beautiful girls, however, find Duke immensely attractive in a 'comfortable' way. Duke's adjustment from romantic lead is a suitable one.

Today, at sixty-three, he's still way ahead leading the field, the world's most popular star. No man can say he hasn't earned it. At an age when most stars have either retired to run businesses or to sink into obscurity, Duke is being offered a million dollars a film. He could sign contracts for the next ten years if he wanted to.

He won't because he wants to be in full control of his work, just as he is of himself. He has never compromised in his life and he isn't going to start now.

John Wayne has experienced most of the fun, fame, fantasy and tragedy possible for a man. It hasn't changed him. He will never retire. As long as people want to see him, Duke will saddle up and ride into that endless sunset. He loves his work with a passion that is rare in this day and age.

'I'm a lucky man, I guess,' he said not long ago. 'I remember the pleasant and humorous things, not the tragedies. Thank God the human mind has little memory for pain and thank God again that I have no memory for it at all.'

I asked Duke once if he was a religious man.

'I'm not religious in one sense perhaps,' he replied. 'But I'm very conscious there must be a Supreme Being. It would be terrible and pointless if there was no hope for man except for his few short years on this earth. It didn't seem so short a few years back but now it's beginning to look awful short. I haven't done half the things I wanted to do.'

If Duke Wayne hasn't yet done half the things he wanted to do, he's done a great deal more than most. He has and will continue to give pleasure to millions. He has raised seven beautiful children and given them an unchanging example they respect and understand. And he's made his wife a happy woman.

His beginnings were humble but he has created in his life a kind of simple yet splendid magnificence. It comes through in his films as it comes through to those who know him. He has lived well, laughed often and loved much. He has gained the respect of intelligent men and the love of little children.

If today he is a living legend it is not only through his work as an actor but through his life as a man. In Duke Wayne's life – as in few others – the legend has become the reality.

APPENDIX:
JOHN WAYNE'S FILMS

Mother Machree	*Fox Films 1927*
Hangman's House	*Fox Films 1928*
Men Without Women	*Fox Films 1929*
Salute	*Fox Films 1929*
The Big Trail	*Fox Films 1930*
Girls Demand Excitement	*Fox Films 1931*
3 Girls Lost	*Fox Films 1931*
Men Are Like That (Arizona)	*Columbia 1931*
Range Feud	*Columbia 1931*
Maker Of Men	*Columbia 1931*
Texas Cyclone	*Columbia 1932*
Two-Fisted Law	*Columbia 1932*
Lady and Gent (The Challenger)	*Paramount 1932*
Ride Him Cowboy	*Warner Brothers 1932*
The Big Stampede	*Warners 1932*
Haunted Gold	*Warners 1932*
Shadow Of The Eagle	*Mascot Serial 1932*
The Hurricane Express	*Mascot Serial 1932*
The Telegraph Trail	*Warners 1933*
Somewhere In Sonora	*Warners 1933*
The Three Musketeers	*Mascot Serial 1933*
Baby Face	*Warners 1933*
His Private Secretary	*Showmen's Pictures 1933*
The Man From Monterey	*Warners 1933*
Riders Of Destiny	*Lone Star/Monogram 1933*
Sagebrush Trail	*Lone Star/Monogram 1933*
Lucky Texan	*Lone Star/Monogram 1934*
West Of The Divide	*Lone Star/Monogram 1934*
Blue Steel	*Lone Star/Monogram 1934*
The Man From Utah	*Lone Star/Monogram 1934*

Randy Rides Alone	*Lone Star/Monogram 1934*
The Star Packer	*Lone Star/Monogram 1934*
The Trail Beyond	*Monogram 1934*
The Lawless Frontier	*Monogram 1934*
'Neath Arizona Skies	*Monogram 1934*
Texas Terror	*Monogram/Republic 1935*
Rainbow Valley	*Monogram 1935*
The Desert Trail	*Monogram/Republic 1935*
The Dawn Rider	*Monogram/Republic 1935*
Paradise Canyon	*Monogram 1935*
Wesward Ho	*Republic 1935*
The New Frontier	*Republic 1935*
Lawless Range	*Republic 1935*
The Oregon Trail	*Republic 1936*
The Lawless Nineties	*Republic 1936*
King Of The Pecos	*Republic 1936*
The Lonely Trail	*Republic 1936*
Winds Of The Wasteland	*Republic 1936*
Sea Spoilers	*Universal 1936*
The Three Mesquiteers	*Republic 1936*
Conflict	*Universal 1936*
California Straight Ahead	*Universal 1937*
I Cover The War	*Universal 1937*
Idol Of The Crowds	*Universal 1937*
Adventure's End	*Universal 1937*
Born To The West	*Paramount 1937*
Pals Of The Saddle	*Republic 1938*
Overland Stage Raiders	*Republic 1938*
Santa Fe Stampede	*Republic 1938*
Red River Range	*Republic 1938*
Stagecoach	*United Artists 1939*
The Night Riders	*Republic 1939*
Three Texas Steers	*Republic 1939*
Wyoming Outlaw	*Republic 1939*
Allegheny Uprising	*RKO Radio 1939*
The Dark Command	*Republic 1940*
The Refuge (Three Faces West)	*Republic 1940*
Seven Sinners	*Universal 1940*
The Long Voyage Home	*United Artists 1940*
A Man Betrayed	*Republic 1941*

Lady From Louisiana	Republic 1941
Shepherd Of The Hills	Paramount 1941
Lady For A Night	Republic 1941
Reap The Wild Wind	Paramount 1942
In Old California	Republic 1942
Flying Tigers	Republic 1942
The Spoilers	Universal 1942
Pittsburgh	Universal 1942
Reunion In France	MGM 1942
A Lady Takes A Chance (The Cowboy and The Girl)	RKO Radio 1943
In Old Oklahoma (War of the Wildcats)	Republic 1943
The Fighting Seabees	Republic 1944
Tall In The Saddle	RKO Radio 1944
Flame Of The Barbary Coast	Republic 1945
Back To Bataan	RKO Radio 1945
They Were Expendable	MGM 1945
Dakota	Republic 1945
Without Reservations	RKO Radio 1946
Angel And The Badman	Republic 1947
Tycoon	RKO Radio 1947
Fort Apache	RKO Radio 1948
Wake Of The Red Witch	Republic 1948
Red River	United Artists 1948
3 Godfathers	MGM 1949
The Fighting Kentuckian	Republic 1949
She Wore A Yellow Ribbon	RKO Radio 1949
Sands Of Iwo Jima	Republic 1950
Rio Grande	Republic 1950
Operation Pacific	Warner Brothers 1951
Flying Leathernecks	RKO Radio 1951
Big Jim McLain	Warner Brothers 1952
The Quiet Man	Republic 1952
Trouble Along The Way	Warner Brothers 1953
Island In The Sky	Warner Brothers 1953
Hondo	Warner Brothers 1954
The High And The Mighty	Warner Brothers 1954
The Sea Chase	Warner Brothers 1955
Blood Alley	Warner Brothers 1955

The Conqueror	*RKO Radio 1956*
The Searchers	*Warner Brothers 1956*
The Wings Of Eagles	*MGM 1957*
Jet Pilot	*Universal International 1957*
Legend Of The Lost	*United Artists 1957*
The Barbarian And The Geisha	*20th Century-Fox 1958*
Rio Bravo	*Warner Brothers 1959*
The Horse Soldiers	*United Artists 1959*
The Alamo	*United Artists 1960*
North To Alaska	*20th Century-Fox 1960*
The Comancheros	*20th Century-Fox 1961*
The Man Who Shot Liberty	*Paramount 1962*
Valance	*Paramount 1962*
Hatari!	*20th Century-Fox 1962*
The Longest Day	*20th Century-Fox 1962*
How The West Was Won	*20th Century-Fox 1963*
Donovan's Reef	*United Artists 1963*
McLintock!	*Paramount 1964*
Circus World	*United Artists 1965*
The Greatest Story Ever Told	*Paramount 1965*
In Harm's Way	*Paramount 1965*
The Sons Of Katie Elder	*United Artists 1966*
Cast A Giant Shadow	*Paramount 1967*
El Dorado	*Universal 1967*
The War Wagon	*Warner Brothers-Seven Arts 1968*
The Green Berets	
Hellfighters	*Universal 1968*
True Grit	*Paramount 1969*
The Undefeated	*20th Century-Fox 1969/70*
Chisum	*Warner Brothers 1970*
Rio Lobo	*20th Century-Fox 1970*

INDEX